THE DILEMMA IN THE CONGRESSIONAL POWER TO ENFORCE THE FOURTEENTH AMENDMENT

Frederick P. Lewis
University of Lowell

University Press
of America™

University Press of America, Inc.
4710 Auth Place, S.E., Washington, D.C. 20023

Library of Congress Catalog Card Number: 80-5096

TABLE OF CONTENTS

TEXT OF THE FOURTEENTH AMENDMENT

SECTION 1. All persons born or naturalized in the United States, and subject to the jurisdiction thereof, are citizens of the United States and of the State wherein they reside. No State shall make or enforce any law which shall abridge the privileges or immunities of citizens of the United States; nor shall any State deprive any person of life, liberty, or property, without due process of law; nor deny any person within its jurisdiction the equal protection of the laws.

SECTION 2. Representatives shall be apportioned among the several States according to their respective numbers, counting the whole number of persons in each State, excluding Indians not taxed. But when the right to vote at any election for the choice of electors for President and Executive and Judicial officers of a State, or the members of the Legislature thereof, is denied to any of the male inhabitants of such State, being twenty-one years of age, and citizens of the United States, or in any way abridged, except for participation in rebellion, or other crime, the basis of representation therein shall be reduced in the proportion which the number of such male citizens shall bear to the whole number of male citizens twenty-one years of age in such State.

SECTION 3. No person shall be a Senator or Representative in Congress, or elector of President and Vice-President, or hold any office, civil or military, under the United States, or under any State, who, having previously taken an oath, as a member of Congress, or as an officer of the United States, shall have engaged in insurrection or rebellion against the same, or given aid or comfort to the enemies thereof. But Congress may by a vote of two-thirds of each House, remove such disability.

SECTION 4. The validity of public debt of the United States, authorized by law, including debts incurred for payment of pensions and bounties for services in suppressing insurrection or rebellion, shall not be questioned. But neither the United States nor any State shall assume or pay any debt or obligation incurred in aid of insurrection or rebellion against the United States, or any claim for the loss or emancipation of any slave; but all such debts, obligations and claims shall be held illegal and void.

SECTION 5. The Congress shall have power to enforce, by appropriate legislation, the provisions of this article.

INTRODUCTION

The national government in the United States does not possess direct authority over the basic civil rights and liberties of American citizens. Such direct authority always has been and largely continues to be the responsibility of the states. In this fact lies the essence of American federalism. Yet state failure to fulfill this responsibility has in the past often led to or accompanied the greatest deficiencies of American liberty and equality.

The enactment of the Fourteenth Amendment after the Civil War expanded national authority to insure liberty and equality. But such expansion has usually seemed to threaten the federal system. This is the dilemma in the Fourteenth Amendment, different aspects of which are examined in the three essays which constitute this book.

The first essay is "The Development of a Constitutional Dilemma." It explores the dilemma's evolution in Supreme Court interpretation and changing American political and social conditions over several decades.

The second essay is "Enforcing the Fourteenth Amendment Against Private Action: The Unsuccessful Search for the Original Intent." It seeks a deeper understanding of the dilemma by making a study of the historical evidence and a comparative examination of previous studies.

"Fourteenth Amendment Liberties from a Pluralist Perspective" is the third and final essay. It offers a new perspective on the amendment which may contain significant potential for resolution of the dilemma.

While each of the essays has its own focus and can stand on its own, they should normally be read in the order presented. It is hoped that, taken together, they cast some useful light on a conflict which extends to the very foundation of the American constitutional system.

This book could not have emerged if I had not, at various times over several years, received different sorts of help from Robert R. Robbins, Mark D. Howe, Archibald Cox, Doris Ingram Lewis and the University of Lowell Research Foundation. I thank them though they are in no way responsible for it.

SECTION I

THE DEVELOPMENT OF
A CONSTITUTIONAL DILEMMA

In the year 1833, the Supreme Court held that the restrictions contained in the first ten amendments to the Constitution of the United States, popularly known as the Bill of Rights, did not apply to state governments, but only to the national government.[1] Therefore, with the exception of the prohibitions against bills of attainder, impairment of contracts, and ex post facto laws which appear in the main body of the Constitution,[2] that document could not be looked to by Americans as a source of legal protection from acts by state governments that denied basic liberties to which many believed they were entitled.

Federal protection did not become available until the passage of the Fourteenth Amendment during Reconstruction, although some early judicial commentary lends a small amount of support to the speculation that sooner or later the federal courts would have found some way to intervene in these matters anyway.[3] Indeed, although federal protection became theoretically available upon passage of the Fourteenth Amendment in the sense that there existed broad and fresh constitutional phraseology upon which interventionist thrusts could be plausibly based, the process took a long while to develop to a point where federal intervention could be termed meaningful. The principal use of the Fourteenth Amendment for many years was in furtherance of the tradition initiated by Marshall under the auspices of the Contract Clause:[4] the Court acted to protect the "liberties" of established property interests against attempts by states to regulate economic affairs.[5]

The use of the Fourteenth Amendment to advance the cause of civil liberties and civil rights has two aspects; Robert Carr has described them as the shield and the sword.[6] Most people who are aware of the Fourteenth Amendment know something of its use as a shield, that is, as a defense in situations where a state seeks to punish someone for failing to comply with its law and the state's action is voided by the Supreme Court on the ground that the law in question is not permitted by the Fourteenth Amendment.

The Amendment's uses as a sword are less well known for many reasons, not the least of which is that until recently, it was rarely used in that manner by the national government. Before the 1940's, the Amendment was seldom utilized as an offensive weapon to seek out and punish those states or private persons that deprive others of their rights, because of a combination of Supreme Court circumscriptions of congressional enforcement power, congressional unwillingness to pass enforcement legislation, and executive reluctance to prosecute and litigate aggressively. But it was not always so.

During Reconstruction, in the wake of the passage of the Thirteenth, Fourteenth, and Fifteenth Amendments, several important and far-reaching pieces of legislation designed to enforce basic civil rights were passed by the Reconstruction Congresses. The Justice Department was created to strengthen their enforcement and the Reports of the Attorney General during the period show that prosecution was undertaken with some vigor.[7] The five major pieces of Reconstruction civil rights enforcement legislation are the Civil Rights Act of April 9, 1866; the Enforcement Act of May 31, 1870; the Enforcement Act of February 28, 1871; the Enforcement Act of April 20, 1871, also known as the Ku Klux Klan Act; and the Civil Rights Act of March 1, 1875.[8]

The Civil Rights Act of 1866 was passed before the final adoption of the Fourteenth Amendment.[9] Thus, the constitutional authority for its passage was felt to lie in the enforcement clause of the Thirteenth Amendment. The "Black Codes" and other legal impediments to equality in many Southern States were viewed as incidents of slavery and thus, as remnants of a status that Congress could totally obliterate.[10] This 1866 Act conferred citizenship upon all persons born in the United States and gave

> such citizens, of every race and color, without regard to any previous condition of slavery or involuntary servitude...the same right...to make and enforce contracts, to sue, be parties, and give evidence, to inherit, purchase, lease, sell, hold and convey real and personal property and to full and equal benefit of all laws and proceedings for the security of person and property.[11]

Its second section provided

> that any person who, under color of any law, statute, ordinance, regulation or custom, shall subject...any inhabitant...to the deprivation of any right secured...by this act or to different punishment or penalties...by reason of his color or race, than is prescribed for white persons... shall be punished by fine not exceeding one thousand dollars, or imprisonment not exceeding one year or both...[12]

The Enforcement Act of 1870 was designed to secure the freedman's equal right to vote, guaranteed by the Fifteenth Amendment,

- 4 -

and set up apparatus toward that end. Its third section provided
for criminal punishment for and civil damages against official action that deprived persons of their right to vote. The fourth
section provided for the punishment of "any person" who attempted
to coerce persons into not voting and the fifth section was aimed
at "any person" who attempts to keep people from voting through
economic coercion such as loss of employment or eviction. Its
important six section was aimed at "two or more persons" who

> conspire together, or go in disguise upon the
> public highway, or upon the premises of another,
> with intent to violate any provision of this act,
> or to injure, oppress, threaten, or intimidate
> any citizen with intent to prevent or hinder his
> free exercise and enjoyment of any right or privi-
> lege granted or secure to him by the Constitution
> or laws of the United States.[13]

There was provision for a fine of up to five thousand dollars and/
or ten years imprisonment. The seventeenth section of this Act
was a slightly modified restatement of section two, the penal section, of the 1866 Act.

The Enforcement Act of February 28, 1871, was a further strengthening of federal controls over elections designed to reinforce the
security of the freedman's right to vote. The Enforcement Act of
April 20, 1871, was an act of exceedingly general scope designed primarily to deal with the growing Ku Klux Klan activity, thus its
popular title, the Ku Klux Klan Act. Its first section provided
that

> any persons who, under color of any law, statute,
> ordinance, regulation, custom or usage of any
> state shall subject...any person to the depriva-
> tion of any rights, privileges, or immunities
> secured by the Constitution of the United States,
> shall...be liable to the party injured in any
> action at law, suit in equity, or other proper
> proceeding for redress...in the several district
> or circuit courts of the United States.[14]

Its second section was a criminal statute providing penalties of
500 to 5000 dollars and jail sentences of from 6 months to 6 years
for conspiracies involving two or more persons who attempt the
overthrow of the United States government's authority, or

who shall conspire together, or go in disguise
upon the public highway or upon the premises of
another for the purpose...of depriving any person or any class of persons of the equal protection of the laws, or of equal privileges or
immunities under the laws, or for the purpose
of preventing the constituted authorities of
any state from giving or securing to all persons
within such state the equal protection of the
laws, or shall conspire together...with intent
to deny to any citizen of the United States the
due and equal protection of the laws, or to injure any person in his person or his property
for lawfully enforcing the right of any person
or class of persons to the equal protection of
the laws...[15]

The third section authorized the President to utilize the armed
forces in "all cases where insurrection, domestic violence, unlawful combinations, or conspiracies in any state" act to interfere with

the execution of the law...as to deprive any
portion or class of the people...of any of the
rights, privileges, or immunities, or protection, named in the Constitution and secured by
this act, and the constituted authorities of
such state shall either be unable to protect,
or shall, from any cause, fail in or refuse
protection of the people in such rights, such
facts shall be deemed a denial by such state
of the equal protection of the laws to which
they are entitled under the Constitution of
the United States;...[16]

The last of the five acts, the Civil Rights Act of March 1,
1895, was what we would term today, a public accommodations act.
It was designed to secure to everyone the equal right to enjoy

the accommodations, advantages, facilities,
and privileges of inns, public conveyances on
land or water, theaters, and other places of
public amusement; subject only to the conditions and limitations established by law, and
applicable alike to citizens of every race
and color, regardless of any previous condition of servitude.[17]

The second section of the Act provided for civil damages and criminal penalties.

These sweeping laws, with the exception of the first one (whose penal section was repassed later on), and those portions of the second and third which rely upon the Fifteenth Amendment's authority, were passed under authority believed to have been established for Congress by the Fourteenth Amendment. However, subsequent Supreme Court decisions indicated that in the Court's eyes, this belief was predominantly incorrect.

Supreme Court Erosion of Congressional Enforcement Power

The first major thrust at the Reconstruction program of civil rights enforcement legislation came with the well-known Slaughter-House Cases.[18] By a close 5-4 vote the Court majority refused to concede that the privileges or immunities of United States citizens (referred to in the first clause of section one after the phrase defining United States citizenship) included anything more than those rights inherent in the existence of the national government.[19] This was done despite the fact that such an interpretation made the clause meaningless since the power to order the states to refrain from interfering with those privileges and immunities inherent in the national government existed even before the passage of the Fourteenth Amendment.[20] Justice Bradley's dissenting opinion[21] points out that before the Fourteenth Amendment, state citizenshop was held primary in America, and the securing of the basic rights of free men which Americans were understood to have derived from their English legal heritage was thus in the hands of the states. However, Bradley argues, since the Fourteenth Amendment now makes national citizenship primary, the national government may surely now prevent the states from violating this broad category of basic rights. He expresses his belief that the privileges or immunities of United States citizens referred to in the Fourteenth Amendment were intended to include all the fundamental rights of citizens, not just the narrow category cited by the majority.

It is true that the general objective sought by the petitioners in the Slaughter-House Cases, that of obtaining recognition of a federal judicial power to set aside set legislation that violates basic rights, was ultimately accomplished by means of the Due Process Clause. But there is one important difference. The due process theory does not claim that the rights protected are federal rights. It recognizes that the responsibility for securing them remains in the hands of the states, but it holds that the requirements of due process prevent the states themselves from violating them.[22] The broad privileges and immunities theory would have accomplished this much, but it would have done so on the premise that the states could not abridge the rights because they were the privileges and immunities of U.S. national citizenship. And as such, as pre-eminently national rights, the federal government could assert the power to protect and secure them, not only from the states, but from private action as well.

Therefore, although not directly at issue in the Slaughter-House Cases, the constitutional support for much of the federal enforcement legislation passed by the Congress was seriously undermined by the Court's refusal to enforce the broad construction of the Privileges and Immunities Clause. Of course, in light of the closeness of the Slaughter-House decision, and the majority's recognition that the Reconstruction amendments were aimed at protecting Negro rights (as distinguished perhaps from the right to open a slaughter-house), matters may have still seemed hopeful at the time.

In 1876, the Court declared unconstitutional sections three and four of the Act of May 1870, because the statute did not restrict its scope to state denial of voting rights that was motivated by color or racial considerations.[23] The implication remained that a more tightly drawn statute would pass muster; however, it should be pointed out that the persons deprived in the case were in fact Negroes.

Perhaps the greatest blow to effective congressional enforcement of basic rights came that same year in U.S. v. Cruikshank.[24] At issue was the scope of section six of the 1870 Act. That Act punished deprivations by anyone of rights or privileges secured by the Constitution and laws of the United States. The Court followed the Slaughter-House majority's approach and refused to agree that the right of assembly was a federal right. It conceded that the right to assemble for the purpose of petitioning Congress for a redress of grievances was "an attribute of national citizenship, and, as such, under the protection of, and guaranteed by the United States."[25] But since the assembly in Cruikshank was not of that nature, the court would not permit the national government to protect it.

The Court in the Cruikshank case further stated,

> The Fourteenth Amendment prohibits a State
> from depriving any person of life, liberty,
> or property, without due process of law; but
> this adds nothing to the rights of one citi-
> zen as against another. It simply furnishes
> an additional guarantee against any encroach-
> ment by the States upon the fundamental rights

which belong to every citizen as a member of
society.[26]

The Court came to the same conclusion regarding the Equal Protection
Clause. Thus the shape of the Court's approach to the Fourteenth
Amendment began to emerge. In addition to adopting the narrow view
of the Privileges and Immunities Clause, the Court would restrict
the scope of the Due Process and Equal Protection Clauses to state
action.

It should be pointed out that in rejecting the claim that the
Fourteenth Amendment's Equal Protection Clause offers relief against
private action in general, the Court stated "there is no allegation
that this [the deprivation of rights] was done because of the color
of the persons conspired against."[27] Again there appeared
the suggestion that narrower protection might be available. These
concessions were probably nods in the direction of those Court mem-
bert who were still unwilling to deny Congress all effective power
to protect Negroes. They also indicate recognition that the Civil
Rights Act of 1866 which confers specific rights upon Negroes re-
lies upon the authority of the Thirteenth Amendment. (That the
Thirteenth Amendment reaches private action was admitted by the
Court, and anti-peonage statutes passed under its auspices have
endured.)[28] Thus for a brief period, the supplementary proposition
that the Thirteenth Amendment authorizes Congress to abolish all
vestiges of slavery by setting forth and then providing protection
for the civil rights of Negroes remained open as a basis for support
of more narrowly drawn enforcement acts;[29] slim possibilities may
also have continued to exist for adoption of more moderate construc-
tions of Congress's powers under section five of the Fourteenth
Amendment. But by 1883, these possibilities were virtually eli-
minated.

In that year the Court declared section two of the Act of April,
1871, unconstitutional because it purported to punish private
action.[30] Those indicted were accused of taking persons from the
custody of state law enforcement officials and lynching them. It
is true that the action of the defendants was not formally alleged
to have been motivated by considerations of race or color. Yet the
fact remains that here was an instance not simply of private citizens coming upon and attacking other, darker skinned private individuals but of a state's having initiated an attempt to provide due
process of law and equal protection of the laws and failing to perform completely these obligations because of private interference.
The Court was clearly not prepared to allow even moderate scope for
enforcement against private individuals. However the Court indicated
in Ex Parte Virginia[31] that it would permit prosecution of state
officials under section five authority and might even be flexible in

determining what constitutes state action. In that case a state
judge excluded Negroes from a jury list. The Court recognized that
the judge acted under color of state authority and that it was not
relevant whether the statutes of the state actually laid down a
discriminatory requirement; it was enough that the judge was an
officer or agent of the state who had, by virtue of his state governmental position, deprived someone of life, liberty, or property
without due process, or of the equal protection of the laws. Such
a person

> as he acts in the name of and for the State,
> and is clothed with the State's power, his
> act is that of the State..[32]

The question of when someone is or is not clothed with the
authority of the state would obviously be of great import in light
of the doctrine that enforcement power under section five would be
limited to improper instances of state action. The distinction is
not always clear. For example, there is a long tradition in Anglo-
American law that certain forms of business, such as the operation
of common carriers or inns, impose special obligations.[33] Might
the operation of such businesses be considered state action? The
answer came in the most thorough statement of the Court's theory of
the Fourteenth Amendment: the opinion in the <u>Civil Rights Cases</u>.[34]
The majority opinion was written by Justice Bradley who had written
a dissenting opinion in the <u>Slaughter-House Cases</u>. This shift sym-
bolized the hardening of the Court's position behind a narrow construction of the Fourteenth Amendment and Congress's powers to enforce it.

At issue was the Civil Rights Act of 1875 and its provisions
forbidding and punishing racial discrimination in places of public
accommodation and recreation. The Court stated that "It is State
action of a particular character that is prohibited. Individual
invasion of individual rights is not the subject matter of the
amendment."[35] The Court recognized that the Amendment was intended
not only to nullify state action of the kind prohibited in the first
section but also in the fifth section, to grant Congress the power
to enforce with appropriate legislation.

> To enforce what: To enforce the prohibition.
> To adopt appropriate legislation for correcting
> the effects of such prohibited State laws and
> State acts, and thus to render them effectually
> null, void, and innocuous. This is the legisla-
> tive power conferred upon Congress, and this is
> the whole of it. It does not invest Congress
> with power to legislate upon subjects which are

within the domain of State legislation; but to
provide modes of relief against State legislation, or State action, of the kind referred to.
It does not authorize Congress to create a code
of municipal law for the regulation of private
rights; but to provide modes of redress against
the operation of State laws, and the action of
State officers executive or judicial, when these
are subversive of the fundamental rights specified...Positive rights..are..secured; but..by..pro-
hibition against State laws..affecting [them], and
by power given to Congress [to carry] such prohibition into effect; and such legislation must
necessarily be predicated upon such supposed
State laws or State proceedings, and be directed
to the correction of their operation and effect.[36]

Thus did the Supreme Court put stringent limitations upon the Fourteenth Amendment and Congress'power to enforce it. The narrow construction of the Privileges and Immunities Clause was retained; the
Court refused to accept the argument that the right to utilize public inns, restaurants, theatres, conveyances, and the like without
regard to race is a privilege or immunity of U.S. citizenship. And
it refused to countenance the proposition that

because the rights of life, liberty, and property [which include all civil rights men have]
are by the amendment sought to be protected
against invasion on the part of the State without due process of law, Congress may provide
for their vindication in every case; and that
because the denial by a State to any persons,
of the equal protection of the laws, is prohibited by the amendment, therefore Congress
may establish laws for their equal protection.[37]

The Court's reason was that to do so would be to clear the way for
the establishment of a code of municipal law regulative of all private rights between man and man in society. It feared that Congress
would "take the place of the State legislatures and...supersede
them."[38] Thus the Amendment was restricted in its coverage solely
to instances of state action, and congressional enforcement power
was limited to punishment of state officials who act to deny these
guarantees. The Court also refused to accept the argument that discrimination of the type at issue is an incident of slavery such as
to permit its prohibition by the Congress under the enforcement
clause of the Thirteenth Amendment.

Justice Harlan's dissent criticized the majority, concluding that "the substance and spirit of the recent amendments of the Constitution have been sacrificed by a subtle and ingenious verbal criticism."[39] He suggested that places of public accommodation and recreation and modes of public conveyance are clothed with a public interest sufficient to warrant their inclusion within the coverage of the Fourteenth Amendment. He also believed that the authority of the Thirteenth Amendment is broad enough to prohibit such discrimination as a vestige or badge of slavery.[40]

The Decline of the National Effort

In the wake of the Civil Rights Cases, the next few decades brought a period of quiescence to the use of federal power to protect basic rights. Except for an occasional successful prosecution on behalf of the very narrow category of rights and privileges the Court was willing to consider a part of United States citizenship, the activities of the Justice Department were minimal, as most Presidents and Attorneys-General lost interest in vigorously pursuing a cause that was, of course, on the practical level primarily of benefit to the Southern Negro. Loss of interest by the executive branch, which was matched and probably exceeded in the legislative and judicial branches, reflected the growing loss of interest in, indeed even hostility to, the cause of the Negro by Northern public opinion, even "liberal" opinion.[41] The Court went so far as to declare that segregation met the requirements of equality contained in the Equal Protection Clause.[42] The Congress began to repeal Reconstruction legislation,[43] a process rendered difficult only by the fact that the Supreme Court had already declared so much of it unconstitutional. The Wilson administration brought racial discrimination to the national civil service in Washington.[44]

However, the cause of national protection of basic rights and liberties did receive one major boost during the post-Reconstruction period. The Court began gradually to support the idea that the Due Process Clause guarantees "certain immutable principles of justice which inhere in the very idea of free government which no member of the Union may disregard."[45] While used initially and for many years primarily by the Court to protect what were viewed as property rights from interference by state regulation, the availability of the Clause to guarantee other political and personal rights and liberties achieved increasing recognition. Of course, had such recognition been achieved under the Privileges and Immunities Clause as the Slaughter-House minority desired, the way would have been clear for direct federal enforcement to protect these rights against all injury, public or private. Again, it must be emphasized that the theory of the Due Process Clause does not really challenge the proposition that these rights and their protection remain incidents of one's state citizenship. It simply imposes a limited, and essentially negative federal obligation upon the states to refrain from taking action that interferes with them. There is no affirmative federal obligation upon the states to assure that no private source interferes with them and since they are not federal rights, no automatic federal power to provide such protection in the event of state inadequacy.

Still the expansion of due process rights went on throughout the early decades of the twentieth century until in the 1937 case of Palko v. Connecticut Justice Cardozo could list the following:

> ...the freedom of speech which the Frist Amendment safeguards against encroachment by the Congress (De Jonge v. Oregon, 299 U.S. 353, 364; freedom of the press (Grosjean v. American Press Co., 297 U.S. 233; Near v. Minnesota, 283 U.S. 697,707) or the free exercise of religion (Hamilton v. University of California, 293 U.S. 245, 262; cf. Grosjean v. American Press Co., 297 U.S. 233, supra; Pierce v. Society of Sisters, 268 U.S. 510), or the right of peaceable assembly, without which speech would be unduly trammeled (De Jonge v. Oregon, 299 U.S. 353, supra; Herndon v. Lowry, 301 U.S. 242 supra), or the right of one accused of crime to the benefit of counsel (Powell v. Alabama, 287 U.S. 45).[46]

The Modern Era

The New Deal of Franklin Roosevelt brought to the Supreme Court a number of Justices sensitive to the problems of civil rights and liberties in America, and the decline in judicial intervention into economic affairs that followed the Court-packing crisis was followed by rising judicial activism in the area of civil liberties.[47]

Congress began to stir and proposals to expand federal protection of basic rights were seriously put forth again. However, Southern influence and filibusters blocked any new major legislation until the 1960's.[48]

In 1939 the Civil Rights Section in the Criminal Division of the Justice Department was created[49] and a serious attempt was made to resuscitate enforcement of the Fourteenth Amendment utilizing whatever could be salvaged from the reconstruction statutes. 42 U.S.C.A. Section 1983 provides for civil remedies; its development was to depend more on the efforts of non-governmental forces. The government found that it had available essentially two statutes: 18 U.S.C.A. section 241 and 18 U.S.C.A. section 242. The former was

originally section 6 of the Act of May 31, 1870, the latter was
section 2 of the Civil Rights Act of 1866.[50]

Section 241 is a conspiracy statute; therefore the offense must
involve two or more people. The statute speaks of rights or privileges secured by the Constitution and laws of the United States;
thus it is applicable to denials of whatever rights the courts
would place in that category against both private and public action.
The category is a regrettably narrow one, but many of the rights
were known to the Justice Department and they proceeded to develop
its coverage.

The Supreme Court as early as 1868 in <u>Crandall v. Nevada</u> had
spoken of the implied federal right of access to the seat of
national government in Washington, to seaports where foreign trade
is conducted and to the national government's land offices, revenue
offices, sub-treasuries and courts of justice.[51] Other cases spoke
of: a federal right to be free from involuntary servitude,[52] a right
to vote in a federal election if qualified (but not in a state
election),[53] the right to be free from physical attack while in
federal custody,[54] the right to enter and hold land free from interference under the Homestead Acts,[55] the right to inform federal
officers of federal offenses,[56] the right to peacefully assemble to
discuss matters pertaining to the activities of the federal government (but not the state government).[57] Lower federal courts have
spoken of rights to give testimony in federal courts, to enjoy access
to federal courts to seek enforcement of federal decrees, and to
perform the duties of federal office without interference.[58]

The most important cases involving use of section 241 have
involved protection of the right to vote in federal elections. They
are <u>U.S. V. Classic</u>[59] and <u>U.S. V. Saylor</u>[60] in which the Court broadened
the definition of the federal election right, extending it to pri-
maries and instances of fraud and ballot box stuffing. The narrow
category of federal rights covered by 241 has limited that statute's
usefulness considerably, despite the fact that it does allow the
national government to reach private action that interferes with
the few recognized federal rights.

Greater interest has surrounded the attempts to activate section 242. Although the language limits offenses to those committed
under color of law, thus excluding private action, the scope of
those federal rights that were recognized as existing against the
states had been broadened considerably over the years through liberal interpretation of the Due Process Clause. Thus the statute
seemed available for prosecution of state officers who denied these
rights. The attempt to establish Section 242 as a weapon against
police brutality produced one of the most confused decisions in

the annals of constitutional law in 1945. No opinion in the case,[61] Screws v. U.S., had the support of more than four of the Justices.

The Court was troubled by the vagueness of offenses covered. After all, the scope of the due process rights recognized by the Courts has hardly been precise and constant. Those who joined in the opinion of the Court felt this criticism was met by reading in the requirement of specific intent, that is, the particular intention in the mind of an offending state official to deny the victim his due process rights as distinguished, evidently, from the negligent or innocent application of excessive force. The Court did not require that the specific intent be formulated in precise constitutional terms. Where the due process right has been clearly spelled out, and state officials nonetheless act with bad purpose or evil intent to deny the right, they may be punished. The Court rejected the argument that since the behavior of the defendant was contrary to the laws of the state he was not acting under color of law. They cited U.S. v. Classic[62] to the effect that "misuse of power, possessed by virtue of state law and made possible only because the wrongdoer is clothed with the authority of state law, is action taken 'under color of' state law." The case was reversed and remanded for retrial under the standards announced.

Three Justices were unwilling to accept the proposition that the action of the sheriff and his cohorts was "under color of law," thus favoring reversal with no further proceedings.[63] One Justice, Murphy, felt that the prosecution was adequate as it stood, and favored affirmance rather than return to the trial court. The final Justice, Rutledge, essentially agreed with Murphy but cast his vote with those who favored reversal and a new trial in order to prevent deadlock. Thus the utility of section 242 in prosecuting state officials who deprive persons of their due process rights has been somewhat impaired by the ambiguity surrounding the standards for its application.

Section 1983,[64] the civil action section, had a development parallel to that of 242. It served as a basis for Smith v. Allright,[65] which led the Supreme Court to outlaw the white primary in Texas even though it was conducted by party officials who were not formally working for the state.

Perhaps most significant was Monroe v. Pape.[66] In a police brutality situation somewhat similar to that in Screws, plaintiffs brought suit against police officers for illegal search and seizure, and illegal detention. The Supreme Court upheld the action under the statute. Furthermore, since the statute was not criminal in nature, the Court found that the stricter requirement of specific intent it had read into section 242 was not necessary here.

- 15 -

Concern for precise standards in criminal prosecutions led a majority of the Court to reject the use of section 241 for similar deprivations that were the result of conspiracies in U.S. v. Williams.[6] Thus section 241 remained useful only for prosecuting conspiracies that deprived persons of those rights already discussed which the national government could protect against both state and private action, but not due process rights. And section 242, which was available against deprivations of due process rights, could be used only if the jury found the requisite specific intent. (The Williams limitation forbidding application of section 241 to instances of state deprivation of Fourteenth Amendment rights was later reversed in U.S. v. Price.[68])

The inadequacy of these statutes was demonstrated dramatically by the upsurge in violence in the South as civil rights activities increased in the late 1950's and early 1960's. It is true, of course, that the problem of maintaining some minimum standard of liberty and security for all members of the American nation in all its parts has been with us since the founding of the United States and is not confined to one region or time. On the other hand it is clear that it was the denial of that minimum to the American Negro by Southern state legal machinery, and the insistence of the larger national community that it be provided, that brought this problem to the fore in recent years.

The record of violence and deprivation of rights is well known. In Law Enforcement — A Report on Equal Protection in the South,[69] the U.S. Commission on Civil Rights cites figures of the Southern Regional Council to the effect that there were a total of 225 incidents of racially motivated violence in the South from January 1955 through January 1959. In only a few cases were any persons arrested or prosecuted by local authorities. Violence increased in 1961 following vigorous Civil Rights activity. In Mississippi alone, from January 1961 to May 1964, there were over 150 serious incidents of racial violence. During the summer of 1964, a time of concerted drive by Civil Rights organizations, there were reports of 35 shootings 30 bombings, 35 church burnings, 50 beatings, and at least 6 murders. Again in only a few cases were those responsible arrested or prosecuted by local authorities.[70]

The Commission focused its study on Mississippi. It found local authorities ineffective in controlling violence and apprehending the responsible parties. In general authorities manifested great hostility toward Negroes and white civil right workers who were victims of violence, treating them as suspects.

They found a general failure of law enforcement due to racially hostile attitudes of police chiefs, sheriffs, and prosecuting attorneys. They further concluded that failure to make prompt arrests and take a stand against violence tended to encourage vigilante action. Federal prosecution under the available statutes could not provide vindication of rights in many instances.[71] It was the problem of providing a basis for sufficient formal power to protect the Southern Negro and his friends that reactivated the dilemma in section five during the 1960's.

The Dilemma Reactivated

In his article, "Constitutional Adjudication and the Promotion of Human Rights,"[72] Professor Archibald Cox points to South Carolina v. Katzenbach[73] as the initial step in the development of a broader interpretation of Congress's section five powers. In that case the Court upheld the Voting Rights Act of 1965 and provided for suspension of state literacy tests wherever less than 50 percent of the adult population had voted in the 1964 Presidential elections. The state challenged Congress's power to provide for such suspensions in the absence of a prior judicial determination of discrimination. The Court rejected this contention, holding that the enforcement clause contained the equivalent of the traditional "necessary and proper" power first spelled out in McCulloch v. Maryland.[74] While the South Carolina case involved a federal statute that attempted to control state activities only (and the Fifteenth rather than the Fourteenth Amendment), Professor Cox points out that if Congress can do whatever it reasonably considers necessary and proper to make sure that states will adhere to their Fifteenth Amendment obligations (and thus certainly also their Fourteenth Amendment obligations),[75] there is no reason why Congress may not find it necessary and proper to regulate certain private activity as well in the belief that such regulation might reasonably promote those obligations.

He believes that most of these logical implications were borne out in the case of Katzenbach v. Morgan.[76] Here the Court sustained that part of the Voting Rights Act which prohibited the denial of the vote on grounds of illiteracy in English to anyone who had completed six years of Spanish language instruction in Puerto Rico. The Court did not insist that Congress could strike down the state's requirement of English literacy because such a requirement was itself violative of the equal protection obligation. Instead they suggested that Congress may have outlawed the requirement because they viewed it as an obstacle to mainland Puerto Rican's obtaining equal state services in public schools, public housing and law enforcement.

Professor Cox's point then is: if Congress may do anything
that might be reasonably related to promoting circumstances that
will aid the citizen in obtaining equality in state services, the
addition to congressional power may be very large indeed. Furthermore he points out that the Fourteenth Amendment also confers
upon citizens the right to be free from interference with life,
liberty and property without due process of law. Arrangements
which some Congress might consider necessary and proper to prevent abridgement of that right could well involve the superces-
sion of much traditional state authority,[77] thus reviving fears
of the sort expressed by the majority in the Civil Rights Cases.

Of course if the traditional doctrine that the federal government's section five enforcement power cannot reach private individuals were reaffirmed, the scope of what could be necessary and
proper would be sizeably reduced and the more extreme possibilities excluded. However, in U.S. v. Guest,[78] a total of six justices, in concurring opinions expressed their belief regarding
that question to the opposite effect.[79]

In the Guest case, the Court found it unnecessary to decide
whether or not section 241, the conspiracy statute, reaches private action or whether it would be constitutional if it did. The
six justices, however, took the unorthodox step of stating that
while it may not be necessary to decide the matter, they wished
to make it clear that, in their opinion, Congress very definitely
does have the power under section five to punish conspiracies
that interfered with Fourteenth Amendment rights--"with or without
state action."[80]

Cox considers three possible ways of distinguishing the power
to punish the type of private action represented by the situation
in the Guest case and the broader power to do whatever is necessary
and proper to secure Fourteenth Amendment rights against either
state or private activity.[81] First, the congressional power could
be confined to prohibited activity that is engaged in for the specific purpose of denying Fourteenth Amendment rights. Thus while
it is easily conceivable that persons might attack a Negro for the
specific purpose of preventing him from enjoying equal (i.e.,
unsegregated) public services, few deprivations of life, liberty
or property by private individuals are undertaken for the specific
purpose of denying the victim his right to have the state refrain
from denying him life, liberty or property without due process.
But Professor Cox believes, sensibly it would seem, that requirement of specific intent is too elusive to stand up, and that it is
even an irrelevant consideration if a person's right to equality
in public education or some other state service is in fact being
interfered with.[82]

- 18 -

A second possible distinction he considers is the limitation of federal power to situations where there is some sort of special relationship between the state and the victim at the time the private interference takes place. Thus a situation resembling that in U.S. v. Harris[83] where a prisoner is taken from the custody of the state by private persons and lynched would be within the federal power but a homicide on the Boston common, even if resulting from racial prejudice, would not involve a special relationship between the victim and the state and would therefore not be subject to federal jurisdiction.[84]

A final and related possibility Cox suggests is that perhaps a distinction can be made in the relative importance to particular situations of the federal right interfered with. In Guest, the deprivation of equality in state services was an important consequence of the private action and central to it. Should Congress pass a law against ordinary theft and if someone were prosecuted under it, the federal right that the statute would be further securing, that of having the state refrain from taking property without just compensation, would be rather remote from the events that lead to prosecution.[85]

However, Professor Cox concludes that these distinctions, which turn on matters of degree rather than on more clear-cut and general criteria, are not likely to serve as the basis necessary for any meaningful restriction of federal power under section five of the Fourteenth Amendment. This conclusion seems justified. An attempt to lay down a line of distinction based upon "practical significance" and "matter of degree" might well lead to recurrent conflict between the two branches if Congress pursued the matter vigorously. The Court would either have to become deeply involved in the business of legislating, something which it should not do, or else face steady erosion of the line laid down. And as Professor Cox points out, one of the probable considerations leading the Court to the expansion of congressional enforcement power in the Fourteenth Amendment area is the growing recognition that problems of equality will increasingly require the fashioning of affirmative solutions, a role for which the Court is not really fitted.[86]

Conclusion: The Dilemma in Temporary Abeyance

Thus it does appear that these distinctions will not mark a way out of the dilemma. Does this mean that we must rely on the fact that under prevailing conditions Congress is not likely to take its powers very far?[87]

Perhaps so. The abrupt termination of the civil rights revolution in the late 1960's, coupled with the Court's sudden resuscitation

- 19 -

in 1968 of the Thirteenth Amendment as a source of authority for legislation to prohibit and punish racial discrimination from any source, has placed the dilemma on the "back burner". This later development may be no accident. Professor Cox's illustration in 1966 of the full implications of the path the Court was taking may have been enough to convince it of the wisdom of pulling back a bit.

In any case, whether the dilemma becomes "relevant" again, and is of more than academic interest, will depend upon whether the Court and the Congress ever find it necessary to consider the protection of basic rights against private interference under legislation of a scope that exceeds the exclusively racial basis provided by the Thirteenth Amendment. One suspects that some day they will.

SECTION I. References

1. Barron v. Baltimore, 32 U.S. (7 Pet.) 243 (1833).

2. U.S. Constitution, Article I, Section 9, Paragraph 3.

3. Calder v. Bull, 3 U.S. (3 Dall.) 386 (1798), Opinions of Justices Chase and Iredell.

4. Dartmouth College v. Woodward, 4 Wheat. 518 (1818).

5. Lochner v. New York, 198 U.S. 45 (1905), Adkins v. Children's Hospital, 261 U.S. 525 (1923).

6. Robert Carr, Federal Protection of Civil Rights (Ithaca, N.Y.: Cornell University Press, 1947).

7. See the Report of the Attorney General (Washington: U.S. Government) for the years 1870 through 1875.

   See also Robert G. Dixon, "The Attorney General and Civil Rights 1870-1964" in Luther A. Huston et al., Roles of the Attorney General of the United States (American Enterprise Institute, Washington, D.C. 1968). Under the administrations of Attorney General Akerman and his successor, "the Enforcement Act of 1870 and the Ku Klux Klan Act of 1871 were vigorously, and imaginatively, enforced," p. 108. This article quotes with approval the following passage from Cummings and McFarland, Federal Justice (New York: Macmillan, 1937) at page 248:

   > Reconstruction had brought upon the Department of Justice tremendous criticism. "The Inflation of the Attorney General" was the title of an article in the Nation in the Autumn of 1874. "The control of the troops in the Southern States," said the article, "has been transferred to the Attorney General, who moves them on the marshall's report." The Attorney General, it continued, "has become a kind of political bureau, to which competitors for the government of sovereign States carry their petitions and proofs. Southern governors now report to him on the State elections, on the general condition of the State, on its finances and taxation, its criminal justice, and take his advice as to internal legislation. Political parties send in to him statements of their grievances, and ask

him for redress against the tyranny or exactions
of the local rulers, and he accepts all the power
and influence which the position brings with equa-
nimity. He snubs the proud, warns the unruly, dis-
courages the wicked, and cheers on the faithful
supporters of the administration."

8. 14 Stat 27; 16 Stat 140; 16 Stat 433; 17 Stat 13; 18 Stat 335.

9. The Civil Rights Act became law on April 9, 1866, while the
Fourteenth Amendment was being formulated. The Amendment
was not finally adopted until 1868.

10. Congressional Globe, 39th Congress, 1st Session (1866), pp. 39,
474, 516-517, 602-603, 1123-1125, 1151-1153, 1160.

11. Act of April 9, 1866, 14 Stat. 27, Section 1, codified in sections 1977 and 1978 of the Revised Statutes of 1874, now 42
U.S.C. 1981 and 1982.

12. This statute is now contained, in essence, in 18 U.S.C. 242.

13. The essence of this statute is still in effect as 18 U.S.C. 241.

14. The core of this section may now be found in 42 U.S.C. section
1983.

15. Act of April 20, 1871, section 2, 17 Stat. 13.

16. Act of April 20, 1871, section 3, 17 Stat. 13.

17. Act of March 1, 1875, section 1, 18 Stat. 335.

18. 83 U.S. (16 Wall.) 36 (1873).

19. The Court speculated on some rights that might be included.
See Brewer v. Hoxie, 238 F. 2d. 91 (8th Cir.) (1956) for a
list.

20. Since the national government existed before passage of the
Fourteenth Amendment, any right inherent in that government's
existence was inherent from the beginning. Crandall v. Nevada,
6 Wall. 35 (1868) was based on a situation which arose before
passage of the Fourteenth Amendment; reversing the conviction
of a stagecoach driver who had refused to pay a tax imposed by

SECTION I. References - (Cont.)

the state on egress from the state, the Court spoke in terms
of federal governmental power to bring its citizens to the
national capital for various purposes, and the correlative
rights of the citizen to come to the capital to assert his
claims, or transact business with the government.

21. 83 U.S. 36, 111-124 (1873).

22. "It [Fourteenth Amendment enforcement power] does not invest
Congress with power to legislate upon subjects which are the
domain of State legislation; but to provide modes of relief
against State legislation, or State action of the kind referred to in the first section of the amendment. Civil
Rights Cases, 109 U.S. 3, 11 (1883)." In Twining v. New Jersey,
211 U.S. 78 (1908) the Court reiterated the Slaughter-House
majority's conclusion that "the civil rights sometimes described
as fundamental and inalienable, which, before the War
Amendments were enjoyed by state citizenship and protected
by state government, were left untouched by this the Privileges and Immunities Clause clause of the Fourteenth Amendment." The Court also rejected the contention that the Clause
specifically included those rights referred to in the national
Bill of Rights, referring to its previous decision in Maxwell
v. Dow, 176 U.S. 581 (1900). But the Court was willing to
consider the possibility that "some of the personal rights
safeguarded by the first eight Amendments against national
action may also be safeguarded against state action, because
a denial of them would be a denial of due process of law."
Thus, for example, the right to free religious exercise would
be protected against federal governmental interference by the
First Amendment, and against state governmental interference
by the Due Process Clause of the Fourteenth Amendment. Hamilton
v. University of California, 293 U.S. 245 (1934). But there
would be no federal protection against private interference
with the right. Any governmental remedies that would be
available in this instance would have to be state remedies.

23. U.S. v. Reese, 92 U.S. 214 (1876).

24. 92 U.S. 542 (1876).

25. 92 U.S. 542, 554 (1876).

SECTION I. References - (Cont.)

26. 92 U.S. 542, 554 (1876).

27. Ibid.

28. Slavery Act of 1866, 14 Stat. 50; Peonage Abolition Act of 1867, 14 Stat. 546.

29. This doctrine has been revived in Jones v. Mayer, 392 U.S. 409 (1968).

30. U.S. v. Harris, 106 U.S. 629 (1883).

31. 100 U.S. 339 (1880).

32. 100 U.S. 339, 347 (1880).

33. See discussion of this matter in Munn v. Illinois, 94 U.S. 113 (1877).

34. 109 U.S. 3 (1883).

35. 109 U.S. 3, 11 (1883).

36. 109 U.S. 3, 11-12 (1883).

37. 109 U.S. 3, 13 (1883).

38. Ibid.

39. 109 U.S. 3, 26 (1883).

40. 109 U.S. 3, 36 (1883). The expansive interpretation of Congress' power to regulate interstate commerce during the 1930's and 40's [see Wickard v. Filburn, 317 U.S. 111 (1942)] cleared the way for re-passage of federal guarantees of non-discrimination in places of public accommodation based upon the now sufficient support of the Commerce Clause. Southern filibusters delayed passage until 1964. 42 U.S.C. section 2000, 78 Stat. 241 (1964).

41. Lerone Bennett, Jr., Confrontation: Black and White (Baltimore: Penguin Books, 1968), p. 77; C. Vann Woodward, The Strange Career of Jim Crow (New York: Oxford University Press, 1966), particularly pp. 67-109; Blaustein and Zangrando, Civil Rights and the American Negro (New York: Washington Square Press, 1968), pp. 283-321; U.S. Civil Rights Commission, Freedom to the Free (Washington: U.S. Government Printing Office, 1963), pp. 55-61.

42. <u>Plessy v. Ferguson</u>, 163 U.S. 537 (1896).

43. Carr, <u>Federal Protection</u>, pp. 4547; <u>Freedom to the Free</u>, p. 55.

44. <u>Freedom to the Free</u>, pp. 84-86; Vann Woodward, <u>Jim Crow</u>,
     p. 93; Bennett, <u>Confrontation</u>, p. 112.

45. <u>Holden v. Hardy</u>, 169 U.S. 366, 389 (1898).

46. 302 U.S. 319, 324 (1937). Time has expanded the list: see
     <u>U.S. v. Arizona</u>, 91 S. Ct. 260, 267, footnote 1 (1970).

47. See G. Theodore Mitau, <u>Decade of Decision</u>, (New York:
     Charles Scribner's Sons, 1967); Milton R. Konvitz,
     <u>Expanding Liberties</u> (New York: Viking Press, 1966);
     Alexander Bickel, <u>The Least Dangerous Branch</u> (Indianapolis:
     Bobbs-Merrill, 1962); Archibald Cox, <u>The Warren Court</u>
     (Cambridge, Massachusetts: Harvard University Press, 1968.

48. Two relatively minor civil rights bills were piloted through
     the Senate in 1957 and 1960 by majority leader Lyndon
     Johnson. The first, 71 Stat. 634 (1957), set up the U.S.
     Commission on Civil Rights as its major contribution and
     made some attempt at protecting further the right to vote
     in federal elections. The second bill, 74 Stat. 86 (1960),
     was primarily concerned with voting and provided for
     preservation of voting records, Court appointed referees
     to look into possible deprivations of voting rights and
     Justice Department action on behalf of aggrieved individual
     voters. While doubtless significant as the first new
     Civil Rights legislation since 1875, the contribution of
     these bills was very small when compared to what followed.

     The 1964 Act dealt with public accommodations, voting,
     public facilities, education and employment. It provided
     broad powers for suits by the Attorney-General on behalf
     of aggrieved individuals and for the cutting off of federal
     funds from non-complying persons or businesses. 78 Stat.
     241 (1964). The 1965 Voting Rights Act provided for the
     appointment of federal registrars to enroll voters in States
     that met a "trigger" test of non-registration. It also
     prohibited these states from making any change in their
     voting laws without prior approval of the Attorney-General
     of the U.S. 79 Stat. 437 (1965). The 1968 Act outlawed
     discrimination in much of America's housing and
     provided more stringent penalties for interference

with the exercise of many civil rights by either state or private action. 82 Stat. 73 (1968).

49. (Now the Civil Rights Division).

50. See Justice Frankfurter's chart of the evolution of these statutes, reproduced in U.S. v. Williams, 341 U.S. 70, 83-84 (1950)

51. 6 Wallace 35, 44 (1868).

52. Smith v. U.S., 157 Fed. 721 (1907), certiorari denied, 208 U.S. 618 (1908).

53. Ex Parte Yarborough, 110 U.S. 651 (1884); U.S. v. Mosely, 238 U.S. 383 (1915).

54. Logan v. U.S., 144 U.S. 263 (1892).

55. U.S. v. Waddell, 112 U.S. 76 (1884).

56. Motes v. U.S., 178 U.S. 458 (1900).

57. U.S. v. Cruikshank, 92 U.S. 542 (1876) (dictum).

58. Foss v. U.S., 266 Fed. 338 (1920); U.S. v. Lancaster, 44 Fed. 885 (1890); U.S. v. Patrick, 54 Fed. 338 (1893). See also Brewer v. Hoxie, 238 F. 2d 91 [8th Cir.] (1956) for a list of implied federal rights.

59. 313 U.S. 299 (1941).

60. 322 U.S. 385 (1944).

61. 325 U.S. 91 (1945). A Sheriff, Policeman, and Special Deputy arrested a young Negro and beat him, inflicting injuries from which he died.

62. 313 U.S. 299, 326 (1941).

63. Frankfurter, Roberts, and Jackson.

64. Sec. 1983. Every person who, under color of any statute, ordinance, regulation, custom, or usage of any State or Territory, subjects, or causes to be subjected, any citizen of the United States or other person within the jurisdiction thereof to the deprivation of any rights, privileges or immunities secured by the Constitution and laws, shall be liable

to the other party injured in an action at law, suit in equity, or other proper proceeding for redress.

65. 341 U.S. 70 (1951).

66. 365 U.S. 167 (1961).

67. 341 U.S. 70 (1951); Williams' conviction under section 242 was upheld in the case of Williams v. U.S., 341 U.S. 97 (1951).

68. 383 U.S. 787 (1966).

69. (Washington, D.C.: U.S. Government Printing Office, 1965.)

70. Law Enforcement, p. 13, citing Southern Regional Council et al., Intimidation, Reprisal and Violence (1959), pp. 15-30; News Release, Voter Education Project, March 31, 1963 (mimeo); U.S. Commission on Civil Rights, Staff Memorandum, "A Chronology of Violence in Mississippi," dated March 23, 1964; Hebers, "Communique from Mississippi," N.Y. Times, November 8, 1964, section six (Magazine), p. 34.

Additional evidence of the violence directed at Negroes in this country, and particularly in the South over the years, is regrettably abundant. See Freedom to the Free, pp. 184-187; Justice, United States Commission on Civil Rights Report (Washington, D.C.: U.S. Government Printing Office, 1961) Violence outside the South directed against Negroes is reported in the N.Y. Times of June 21, 1961; August 10, 1961; June 21, 1962; April 18, 1963; August 1, 2, 3, 4, 6, 1963; October 7, 1964; July 8, 1965.

The climate of fear was not dispelled from the South in the early 1970's. See Taylor Branch, "Black Fear: Law and Justice in Rural Georgia," in The Washington Monthly, January, 1970, pp. 39-58. See also, "S.C. Mob Attacks School Buses," Boston Globe, March 4, 1970, p. 1.

While the late 1970's have seen less media attention to the problem, that which has been publicized often involves areas of the country outside the South. For example, Boston has seen whites attack black children visiting the site of the Bunker Hill Monument. No convictions have been obtained in the state courts.

71. Fiscal years 1964-65.

Matters rec'd[a]	Cases Presented to Grand Jury	Disposition by Grand Jury		Disposition at Trial	
		No True Bill	Indictment	Acquittals	Convictions
Sect. 241	60	6	1	2	0	0
Sect. 242	4,478	73[b]	37	26	15[c]	6

---

[a]complaints which the FBI by request or previous standing arrangement with the Civil Rights Division has investigated or any other matter docketed on request of an attorney.

[b]three of these actually commenced by filing of information.

[c]in addition, there was one mistrial and three others where the indictments were dismissed.

From Law Enforcement, p. 118. "The present criminal remedies available to the Federal Government to prevent racial violence... are inadequate;" Ibid., p. 175.

72. Harvard Law Review, Vol. 80 (1966), p. 91.

73. 383 U.S. 301 (1966).

74. 17 U.S. (4 Wheat.) 316, 421 (1819). "Let the end be legitimate, let it be within the scope of the constitution, and all means which are appropriate, which are plainly adapted to that end, which are not prohibited, but consist with the letter and spirit of the constitution, are constitutional."

75. Amendment XIV, Section 5. The Congress shall have power to enforce, by appropriate legislation, the provisions of this article

Amendment XV, Section 2. The Congress shall have power to enforce this article by appropriate legislation.

SECTION I.   References - (Cont.)

76. 384 U.S. 641 (1966).

77. Cox, "Foreword," p. 115.

78. 383 U.S. 745 (1966).

79. Clark, joined by Black and Fortas, 383 U.S. 745, 762. Brennan joined by Warren and Douglas, 383 U.S. 745, 782.

80. 343 U.S. 745, 762 (1966).

This unusual behavior can be explained by the fact that the Court was doubtless aware that Congress was then considering proposals to protect minorities and civil rights workers from private violence. Many of these proposals were ultimately included in the Civil Rights Act of 1968, 82 Stat. 73; the constitutionality of parts of this statute cannot be relied upon without section five power to reach private action. Consider for example Title I (b) (1) (A) and Title I (b) (2) (A) and (b) which cover interference by private persons with rights in state elections, schools, colleges, benefits, services, privileges, programs, facilities, or activities on account of race, color, religion or national origin (or in the case of elections, private interference-period). Even the broad expansion of Thirteenth Amendment power in Jones v. Meyer, 392 U.S. 409 (1968) cannot, one assumes, support prosecution of such interference because of religion or national origin. However, the matter has not been tested.

81. Cox, "Foreword," pp. 115-119.

82. Ibid., p. 116.

83. 106 U.S. 629 (1883).

84. Cox, "Foreword," pp. 116-117.

85. Ibid., p. 117.

86. Ibid., pp. 83, 114.

87. Wickard v. Filburn, 317 U.S. 111 (1942) and related cases gave Congress enormous power under the Interstate Commerce Clause, Article I, Section 8 (3), but the Congress has not seen fit to preempt the states to anywhere near the degree possible.

SECTION II

ENFORCING THE FOURTEENTH AMENDMENT AGAINST PRIVATE ACTION:
THE UNSUCCESSFUL SEARCH FOR THE ORIGINAL CONGRESSIONAL INTENT

As is the case with many human enterprises, the development of American constitutional law has had its share of "imagining the past and remembering the future."[1] Much of the former effort has focused on that remarkable period of our history known as Reconstruction. As the United States Supreme Court has, in recent decades, undertaken to undo some of the damage done to the rights of Black Americans in the latter part of the nineteenth century, it has found it useful to broaden or overrule its previous interpretations of the impact of the enactment of the Thirteenth, Fourteenth and Fifteenth Amendments upon our constitutional law,[2] and to resuscitate long dormant enforcement statutes passed by Reconstruction Congresses under powers believed granted by these amendments.[3] To help justify this process, the Court has seen fit to expend considerable energy upon a perusal of the recorded debates of the Reconstruction Congresses and related documents in a search for the original congressional intent.[4]

One of the most investigated matters has been the scope of Congress' power to enforce the well known broad guarantees of the Fourteenth Amendment's first section, particularly whether or not the general statement of Congressional enforcement power contained in section five can reach private action.[5] The Court said "no" in the 1883 Civil Rights Cases[6] but scholars have never taken this as the final word on the subject. Indeed, in 1966 a numerical majority of justices indicated in U.S. v. Guest[7] that they were prepared to hold that section five did allow Congress to reach private action. However, resuscitation and broad interpretation of Congress' powers under the Thirteenth Amendment, coupled with the changed political climate, have permitted the Court to avoid formal adjudication of the question. And with the change in Court personnel over the past decade, one cannot assume that the dicta of Guest would now become law.

But if the issue is not currently a burning one it continues to smolder. The ultimate cause of concern with the question of whether or not Congress can reach private action under section five is the revolutionary potential for altering American federalism which is contained in the interpretation that permits an affirmative answer. This potential was described by Justice Bradley in the Civil Rights Cases[8] as one which would allow the enactment of a superceding federal code of municipal conduct. Movement by the Court in the 1960's toward broad interpretation of Congress' enforcement powers led Professor Archibald Cox to similar conclusions.[9]

Anyone struggling with this tension between the federal Congress' authority to define and protect the basic civil rights of Americans and the traditional scope of state authority will inevitably be brought back to the events of the post-Reconstruction era, and to a series of Supreme Court decisions which constricted the scope of the Amendment and Congress' enforcement powers in ways which cut the ground from under efforts by Congress and the lower federal courts to expand and protect the rights of the newly freed slaves. But while this effort to go to the original intent of the framers of the Fourteenth Amendment for guidance is understandable, it is an exercise that cannot succeed.

Of course it is traditional legal practice when faced with a problem of statutory interpretation that cannot be settled by the "plain words" of the law to return to the record of its framing in search of the original intent. And the Fourteenth Amendment is firmly rooted in the peculiar conditions of the Reconstruction era; one certainly cannot altogether understand it, its enforcement powers or the conflict with state authority which they suggest, apart from the period of formulation.

However, this understanding cannot extend to the point of yielding a concise original intent which could serve as a guide to judicial interpretation. To show why this is so, I have undertaken to examine the evidence in the historical record and some of the different scholarly studies that have interpreted this evidence in an attempt to reconstruct Congress' original intent. Comparison is interesting, for the studies differ from each other to a very great degree. Doubtless this is due in part to contradictions in, and the somewhat opaque nature of, the historical record; one can find some support for almost any position there. Doubtless it is due as well to the fact that at least some of those undertaking historical research in this area did so as advocates seeking support for a pre-ordained conclusion.

But my own study leads me to suggest that the ultimate reason why there is no agreement on the original intent of Congress as to its power to enforce the Fourteenth Amendment against private action is that there was no clear-cut original intent; that is, two-thirds of the Congress which passed the Amendment did not share any intent in that regard. Furthermore, it does not appear that the constitutional majority consisted of differing views which can be compromised.

In attempting to demonstrate this, I undertake not only to dissuade justices and scholars from further efforts to resolve this particular constitutional question by seeking the original intent, but also to suggest it is reasonable to assume that political conditions encouraging ambiguity in the legislative product are not something that was unique to the Reconstruction Congresses; that such conditions frequently prevail both in Congress and in the state legislatures. Poor draftsmanship sometimes may be the cause of vague statutory wording. But it is at least as likely that such vagueness results from the fact that, absent a clear majority intent, ambiguous phraseology is utilized to obscure differing objectives, achieve the necessary majority and obtain a legislative product, with the resultant vagueness dismissed as either inconsequential or something to be worried about by the courts at a future time.

Original Intent: The Record of the Framing

What does the historical record say about whether or not the general statement of congressional enforcement power contained in section five of the Fourteenth Amendment was intended to permit enforcing its first section against private action? The officially documented record of the framing of section one raises more questions than it answers. On its face, it indicates that an Ohio Congressman named Jonathan Bingham was the prime mover in the creation and adoption of section one of the Fourteenth Amendment. A dedicated Abolitionist and prominent Radical Republican leader, Bingham claimed that his efforts were motivated by his personal doubts (unique among Radical Republicans) about the constitutionality of the Civil Rights Bill of 1866.[10] That Bill was enacted under the authority of the second section of the Thirteenth Amendment.[11] But at the time of passage, Bingham stated that he did not believe section two authorized Congress to enact penalties that would apply within the states. Many state laws would be overruled by the bill. It would, for example, be a penal offense against the Unites States for state judges to obey the laws of their states, in Bingham's opinion.[12]

The Bill was ultimately passed with the penal previsions intact, though some of the general language that Bingham had objected to in the proposed first section was removed. The Bill originally stated that there should be "no discrimination in civil rights or immunities among the inhabitants of any State...on account of race, color or previous condition of slavery."[13] Bingham maintained that "civil rights" includes every right that pertains to the citizen including political rights, and he was concerned because almost every state in the union, including his own, restricted the franchise to whites. Largely because of his protests the phrase was removed, though proponents of the Bill did not believe that it was materially changed.[14]

When the final vote came, Bingham was one of only six Republicans in the House recorded as voting against the Bill.[15] When the House overrode President Andrew Johnson's veto, Bingham was paired to support it.[16]

While these events were taking place, Bingham had been appointed to the Joint Committee on Reconstruction which had been formed at the instigation of Senator Thaddeus Stevens of Pennsylvania to act as a sort of "politburo"[17] that would facilitate the enactment of the Radical program over the anticipated opposition of the President. Here, it seems, Bingham sought to create the constitutional authority for the Civil Rights Bill which he believed to be absent.

The Journal of the Joint Committee indicates that when it met for business on Tuesday, January 9, 1866, the first constitutional proposal considered was one of Stevens' that provided for apportioning Representatives on the basis of the number of legal voters as ascertained by a congressional census.[18] Other propositions were also introduced with varying language, but all directed towards the end of having congressional representation vary with the actual percentage of the population of a state that was permitted to vote.

The Joint Committee was then presented with two proposals that had been submitted earlier; one from Bingham and one from Stevens. They were both sent to subcommittee. Bingham's read:

> The Congress shall have power to make all laws
> necessary to secure to all persons in every
> state within this Union equal protection in
> their rights of life, liberty and property.[19]

Stevens' proposal was that

> all laws, state and national, shall operate impar-
> tially and equally on all persons without regard
> to race of color.[20]

Stevens' was presented along with two other articles that focused on suffrage. On February 10, 1863 the Committee sent to the House the following proposed by Bingham as a new constitutional amendment:

> Congress shall have power to make all laws which
> shall be necessary and proper to secure to the
> citizens of each State all privileges and

immunities of citizens in the several States (Art.
4, Sect. 2); and to all persons in the several
States equal protection in the rights of life,
liberty and property (5th Amendment).[21]

The House considered this first Bingham proposal on February
26th.[22] A motion to postpone consideration was passed with the
Republican party, including Bingham, supporting postponement overwhelmingly.[23] The proposal did not return to the floor of Congress
in any form for an extended period. It was during this time that
the Civil Rights Bill of 1866 was passed over Congressman Bingham's
objections of unconstitutionality and President Johnson's veto.

The Committee spent the rest of February and early March on
other matters, primarily questions surrounding the readmission of
Tennessee. After a period of adjournment, it met again in mid-
April. At that time, Stevens introduced a new five-part reconstruction plan which he claimed not to have authored but which he
supported. Much of it was concerned with suffrage. But its first
section did provide:

> No discrimination shall be made by any State nor
> by the United States as to the civil rights of
> persons because or race, color or previous con-
> dition of servitude.

Bingham proposed changing the first section by adding:

> nor shall any state deny to any person within
> its jurisdiction the equal protection of the
> laws, nor take private property for public use
> without just compensation.[24]

Stevens supported the addition, but it did not carry. However
Bingham later proposed to substitute as the proposal's fifth
section:

> No state shall make or enforce any law which
> shall abridge the privileges or immunities of
> citizens of the United States; liberty, or
> property without due process of law, nor deny
> to any person within its jurisdiction the
> equal protection of the laws.[25]

And this proposal was overwhelmingly adopted.

But on April 25, without explanation, the committee voted to
strike out Bingham's proposal. Stevens voted "no" along with
Bingham, but the provision was removed.[26] Bingham attempted to
get his provision adopted as a separate constitutional amendment
but to no avail.[27]

On April 26, Stevens led efforts to make several more
changes in his own reconstruction plan including the addition of
language stating explicitly that if the franchise was denied to
any portion of the male citizenry, the number of House seats
apportioned to that state would be reduced proportionately.[28]

Shortly thereafter, Bingham proposed that the following be
substituted for section one:

> No state shall make or enforce any law which shall
> abridge the privileges or immunities of citizens
> of the United States; now shall any State deprive
> any person of life, liberty or property, without
> due process of law, nor deny to any person within
> its jurisdiction the equal protection of the laws.[29]

This time he succeeded.

The entire proposal was sent to the Congress in essentially
the form in which it was ultimately adopted as the Fourteenth
Amendment. The only change in the wording of section one as
finally adopted by the Committee was the addition of the sentence:
"All persons born or naturalized in the United States, and subject
to the jurisdiction thereof, are citizens of the United States
and of the State in which they reside." The phrase clarified
and reversed the unpopular decision of Chief Justice Taney in
Dred Scott v. Sanford.[30]

This formal record of the framing of section one is hardly
self-explanatory and even when supplemented with other material,
those who have studied it previously have arrived at sharply differing conclusions about the original intent. However, when considered together, these very differences serve to case light on
some of the ambiguities that surround the formal record and
greatly facilitate a better understanding of the evidence.

Original Intent: Putting the Civil Rights Bill of 1866 into the
Constitution.

Examining the evidence available in the congressional debates
is inconclusive, not only because it supports contradictory conclusions but because there is really very little of it. Most of

Congress' attention was centered on sections other than section one. One approach suggests itself immediately, however. Both opponents and supporters maintained that the purpose of section one was to put the guarantees of the Civil Rights Bill of 1866 into the Constitution. The major commentators agree on this point.[31] But, as the review of the formal record indicated, it was disputed at the time of passage and, unfortunately, it remains unclear just what the scope of the Civil Rights Bill of 1866 was intended to be and exactly what possible constitutional deficiencies required correction. In particular, it is uncertain whether the enforcement or penal provisions of the Bill reached private action.

These provisions speak of denial of rights under "color of law...or custom." This language has never been held to reach private action, although some have expressed the opinion that it should be viewed that way.[32] The companion bill to amend the Freedman's Bureau Act speaks of "prejudice" as well;[33] denial of rights rooted simply in prejudice would appear to include private acts. It could be argued that one should look to this companion Act for clear indication of what Congress had in mind in the Civil Rights Bill. It can also be argued that since the Freedman's Bureau Act is so much more explicit, the absence of similar phrasing in the Civil Rights Bill indicates lack of intent to reach private action there. In any case, the "agreement" that section one of the Fourteenth Amendment was designed to put the guarantees of the Civil Rights Bill into the Constitution fails to shed any real light on the original intent as to Congress' own enforcement powers.

Original Intent: The Declared Purposes of Congressman Bingham

Another approach is implicit in the first major study of the Fourteenth Amendment's framing, The Adoption of the Fourteenth Amendment[34] by Horace Flack. Flack's work considers the history of each section and analyzes the events that he deems relevant. To the extent that he deals with the problems of this study, he focuses on Bingham's later claims[35] that his Amendment supports the most far reaching Reconstruction legislation. Flack accepts at face value Bingham's insistence that his second and ultimately adopted formula was just as strong as his first, rejected proposal despite the seemingly less vigorous language of the second proposal.

Since Bingham appears to have been the author of section one, his explanation of its meaning must carry great weight. Nevertheless, it does not follow that the other Committee members shared his particular views as to the nature of that section, its importance, or the problems with which it was meant to deal. Unquestionably Bingham's prime concern, that the Civil Rights Bill in 1866 was unconstitutional and must be legitimized, was not shared by most of his colleagues; Bingham's constitutional views were unique, and this must be kept firmly in mind.[36] Beyond this, it certainly does not follow that the two-thirds of the members of both Houses of Congress, who altered and shaped the Committee's proposal and finally passed it as the Fourteenth Amendment, all shared Bingham's views or even the views of the Committee majority. And if there is in fact a determinable legislative intent in regard to the scope of Congressional power to enforce the Amendment, it is in the minds of the Congressmen who provided the 2/3 majority for the Amendment as finally enacted, that this intent must be authoritatively found.[37]

Members of the Committee separately or together may well have had express or secret reservations about what they proposed.[38] But Committee records are studied because they offer clues to the congressional intent, and if in fact Congress does not share their views, particularly as to broad and ambiguous phrases, then it cannot plausibly be maintained that they are nevertheless binding on Congress. One may well agree with Flack that Bingham, the principal author of section one, intended that section as a firm basis for whatever action Congress deemed necessary and proper to make sure that the states offered and all Americans received, equally, protection of their basic rights (roughly defined as those contained in the Bill of Rights). After all, Bingham said so.[39] But the important question remains not "what did Bingham intend?" but "what did Congress intend?"

While he recognizes that many of the changes made were designed to render the plan more palatable, Flack interprets them simply as an attempt by the Joint Committee to increase drastically the power of the federal government, but to do so in a way that people could not understand. This is probably true; however, it also suggests the likely possibility, given the ambiguities, that Congress too did not understand what the Committee was trying to accomplish, and if so, that it did not intend the Amendment to have a radical construction.

Original Intent: To Explicitly Express the "Natural Rights" Theory of the Constitution

Jacobus TenBroek's work constitutes the most impressive effort to provide support for the proposition that sections one and five together were intended by Congress to do in essence what

Bingham claimed for them and that congressional power under them
is as great as it would have admittedly been if Congress had
passed Bingham's first proposal.[40] TenBroek marshalls abundant
evidence in support of the proposition that the Abolitionists
and then the Radical Republicans were possessed of a particular
ideology which he terms the natural rights theory; and that the
arguments of the Abolitionists, the Fourteenth Amendment itself,
and the legislation passed for its enforcement in the 1870's
should all be viewed as the steady development and expression of
a coherent, if radical, constitutional philosophy.

TenBroek looks at the anti-slavery background of the framers
of the Fourteenth Amendment and points out that they must have
been aware of the threat which private violence may present to
the exercise of civil rights and the need to protect against it.
Reports of conditions that existed in the South in the late 1860's
support TenBroek's view and illustrate that Reconstruction legislation and amendments were passed against a background of state
and private persecution of Negroes.[41]

Overwhelming evidence shows that most framers of the Amendment were possessed of a natural rights ideology which strongly
influenced their labors.[42] It was a major tenet of Abolitionist-
Radical thought that the Constitution as it stood in 1866, if properly interpreted, bound all American governments, state and
national, to respect the rights of all men. They took the Declaration of Independence literally: "all men are created equal; to
secure these rights governments are instituted among men."[43] Thus
many Radicals viewed the Fourteenth Amendment as largely "declaratory": a reaffirmation of principles that were already in the
Constitution.

The Radicals profoundly disagreed with the Supreme Court decisions which asserted that the Bill of Rights was simply a group
of prohibitions against the exercise of certain powers by the
federal government and placed the responsibility for securing the
basic rights of free men with the states. Though they rejected
this view, the Radicals dealt with it by adding the Citizenship
Clause[44] to the beginning of section one of the Fourteenth Amendment. This clause reversed the priorities in American citizenship and made national citizenship primary, with state citizenship dependent simply on where an American citizen chooses to
live. Thus the argument follows, and was made in the Slaughter-
House Cases[45] that since national citizenship is now primary, it
is the national government which now bears the prime obligation
(and thus the power) to secure the "basic rights of free men."
This is a potent argument and four justices accepted it in the
Slaughter-House Cases. But the narrow majority, unwilling to

accept the obvious potential consequences for the federal system, rejected it. If the Privileges and Immunities Clause were broadly defined and protection of all basic rights of Americans viewed as "social contractual" obligations of the federal government, it would follow that the federal government can and must prevent the states from interfering with these rights and that the federal government can and must prevent private individuals from interfering with them.[46]

The Natural Rights Theory and Its Implications

The implications of the natural rights theory cannot be understood if one begins from a perspective of established legal interpretation of the Amendment. For example, today's important distinction between private action and state action was not originally at issue in disputes over congressional enforcement power. The distinction is not relevant to natural rights thinking, for if the obligation to provide certain civil rights protection flows from the national government's obligation to its citizens in return for their loyalty to it, then the government has the power to protect the citizen's rights against any threat, be it from a private source or the actions of state or local governments. Indeed, while the Supreme Court still adheres to the position of the Slaughter-House majority that the privileges and immunities which flow from the U.S. citizenship are a much narrower category than the basic rights of free men which the Radicals envisioned, they have accepted the natural rights logic regarding those few rights which they have seen fit to recognize as flowing from national citizenship; no distinction has ever been made between state and private action that interfered with these rights.[47]

But the TenBroek interpretation and its implicit assumptions cannot be accepted. Granted most Radicals seem to have shared the precepts of what TenBroek calls the "natural rights philosophy" and thus, a broader view of the privileges and immunities of United States citizens than the Supreme Court's Slaughter-House majority chose to validate. Doubtless there would not have been clear agreement as to the outer limits of the rights secured,[48] but most would probably have viewed them as essentially encompassing "life, liberty and property" as then traditionally understood. But the rest of TenBroek's thesis cannot be sustained.

When the historical facts of the framing are put in perspective, they suggest that the Committee's development of a civil rights section actually lacked the clarity of purpose which he suggests. Historical development has made section one very important; the other sections have proven unimportant and it is not

surprising that orderly scholars tend to organize their work topi-
cally and study first one section and then the other. In one
place TenBroek isolates and presents a long list[49] of the various
civil rights section proposals to demonstrate that, despite what
he sees as phrasing disputes between proponents of affirmative
phrasing and those favoring a narrower, negative prohibition,
there was a continuous and consistent attention to the matter.
But Joseph James demonstrates convincingly in his broad study[50] of
the framing of the Amendment that the dominant concern by far of
the framers was not civil rights but rather the problem of suffrage. Indeed if one reads the record of the Joint Committee's
transactions with James' study in mind, the inference becomes
strong that many of the Committee's peculiar and inexplicable
actions in regard to the development of civil rights proposals had
their roots in the conflict over the critical suffrage question.

It hardly seems likely, after all, that Thaddeus Stevens
would support what TenBroek calls "the narrow line of development'
since Stevens was not known for his moderation. Indeed since
virtually no one other than Bingham seemed seriously concerned
with the alleged unconstitutionality of the Civil Rights Act of
1866, and in light of the considerable documentation that Stevens'
prime concerns as Radical Republican leader were the pressing
political questions,[51] since Bingham was obviously concentrating
on the matter of civil rights, it is mildly surprising that
Stevens bothered to submit civil rights proposals at all.

One possible explanation is that the competition between
Bingham's and Stevens' proposals did not center on the question
of affirmative versus negative language; consider the fact that
Bingham's proposals focused specifically on phrases that had
customarily been utilized to encompass the traditional idea of
civil rights while Stevens' proposals spoke of "all laws"
(emphasis added). In light of Stevens' concern with suffrage,
it is possible that he hoped that "all laws" might be stretched
to include voting laws. This possibility gains force when viewed
along with Bingham's expressed opposition during the debate over
the Civil Rights Bill of 1866 to civil rights language that might
be used to confer suffrage upon Negroes.

Although most studies treat congressional debate of the Civil
Rights Bill of 1866 separately for reasons of organization, the
proper perspective is that most of these various constitutional
proposals bearing on the question of both civil rights and suffrage were introduced and considered by the Committee in the
period from December 1865 through April 1866, and the Civil
Rights Bill was debated in Congress in March, 1866. Interesting

too was the fate of Bingham's second major "rights" proposal in the Committee. First it was adopted as part of a new Stevens Reconstruction Plan; then it was removed by the Committee.[52] But after Stevens moved to alter significantly his suffrage proposal, Bingham's second rights proposal was again adopted overwhelmingly by the Committee as part of the Stevens plan, strongly suggesting that the fate of the Bingham civil rights proposal was tied to the politics of the suffrage question. Certainly TenBroek's picture of the Joint Committee as possessed of a specially focused, deliberate and purposeful intent to write the natural rights theory into the Constitution, with just a few technical disagreements over wording, does not seem justified.[53]

Nevertheless, despite the record, which suggests that the development of section one was rather haphazard and lacking in clear direction, TenBroek is correct in viewing the ultimate result as a constitutional statement of the Radical natural rights philosophy. And it is true that this statement was passed and ratified as an amendment to the Constitution. However, this does not settle the matter, for while Congress may well have been aware that it was passing a provision which reflected the natural rights theory in a general way, there were implications in the Radicals' theory which were clearly unacceptable to large segments of congressional opinion. Indeed there is evidence of explicit opposition to the untrammeled Radical position and evidence that alterations were made to accommodate it.

Obstacles to the Uncritical Acceptance of the Natural Rights Theory

The clearest evidence is the rejection by the Congress of Bingham's first major proposal[54] which would have clearly conferred upon the Congress the power to make "all laws necessary and proper to secure to all persons equal protection in the rights to life, liberty and property." This initial proposal presumably best reflects Bingham's views as to what an amendment dealing with human rights should contain. Had it been adopted, its clear, affirmative wording would leave no question about the power of Congress to punish private action. By contrast, the later Bingham proposal that was ultimately adopted as section one of the Fourteenth Amendment contained negative language. The Fourteenth Amendment's first section prohibits the states from doing certain things and then in section five says that Congress may enforce. In 1871, Congressman James Garfield, later President, argued in an exchange with Bingham that these events clearly demonstrate that Congress rejected the broad approach indicated in Bingham's first proposal in favor of the narrower approach of the proposal that was ultimately adopted.[55] Others have found these events similarly significant.[56]

But Bingham rejected Garfield's interpretation. He insisted that when his first proposal was introduced he misunderstood the existing constitutional situation.[57] And his recorded statements in debate at the time indicate that this was so. He apparently believed that states were constitutionally bound to protect basic rights, but that what was absent was constitutional authority enabling Congress to force them to perform this obligation.[58] He appears to have misinterpreted Barron v. Baltimore.[59] This was not an unusual sort of error; accurate legal information was much harder to obtain in 1866 than it is today.[60] Furthermore, there is reason to believe that Bingham and the other framers were aware of and operated under the influence of two important Supreme Court decisions: Kentucky v. Dennison[61] and Prigg v. Pennsylvania.[62] These cases dealt with "An Act Respecting Fugitives from Justice and Persons Escaping from the Service of Their Master," 1 Stat. 02 (1793). The Act was passed by Congress on the assumption that it had the power to enforce the provisions of Article IV of the Constitution which read as follows:

Section 2

(2) A person charged in any State with Treason, Felony, or other Crime, who shall flee from Justice, and be found in another State, shall on demand of the executive Authority of the State from which he fled, be delivered up to be removed to the State having Jurisdiction of the Crime.

(3) No person held to Service or Labour in one State, under the Laws thereof, escaping into another, shall, in Consequence of any Law or Regulation therein, be discharged from such Service or Labour, but shall be delivered up on Claim of the Party to whom such Service or Labour may be due.[63]

These two clauses are essentially similar, except that one applies to fugitives from justice and the other applies to fugitive slaves. They were surely intended to bind the states, to deal with "state action."[64] Yet the provision of the congressional statute which elaborated the directive of paragraph (2) and reaffirmed the duty of the executive authority to extradite fugitives was declared by the Court to impose only a moral duty.[65] The language of the case cast considerable doubt on the power of Congress to bind state officials without explicit constitutional authorization.[66]

On the other hand, in Prigg v. Pennsylvania, the Court upheld
those provisions of a statute passed pursuant to paragraph (3)
which imposed a legal obligation upon private persons to restore
fugitive slaves to their owners and a punishment if they did not.
"If...the constitution guarantees the right...the natural inference certainly is that the national government is clothed with the
appropriate authority and functions to enforce it."[67]

With their personal histories of anti-slavery activity, the
Republican leaders must have been aware of these decisions. Thus,
it is reasonable to assume that they must have believed that once
a right was recognized in the Constitution, Congress automatically
had the power to enforce it against private interference; and that
the major concern of a Congress which desired to secure certain
rights would have to be the effective binding of the states and
their officials.[68]

At the time of his first proposal Bingham seems to have believed that the Bill of Rights did bind the states, but that only
the faithfulness of the states ensured its operation, with no way
of compelling their obedience.[69] Thus, not only did he misunder-
stand Barron v. Baltimore, but he seems to have confused it with
Kentucky v. Dennison.[70]

Initially the text of the first proposal contained specific
references to portions of the Constitution.[71] That supports
Bingham's later position that his intention was merely to fill in
what he thought was missing from existing constitutional prohibitions that formally secured citizens' rights: power in Congress
to enforce.[72]

However, the affirmative language of the proposal did become
an issue in congressional debate. Some alleged that the proposal
would enable Congress to override all state "codes of civil and
criminal jurisprudence and procedure, affecting the individual
citizen" and replace them with its own laws.[73]

It appears that in the end Bingham's first proposal was not
really satisfactory to anyone. As an unconditional grant of power
to Congress, it was not pleasing to moderates. Its failure to act
as a permanent restraint on the states made it undesirable in the
eyes of many Radicals.[74] Throughout this period, many Radicals
recognized that their dominance of Congress might well be temporary.
Future Congresses might not only undo what the Radical Congress had
enacted; they might utilize such power to enact some undesirable
measures of their own. Thus Bingham, after being enlightened[75]

about <u>Barron v. Baltimore</u>, and those Radicals who already understood the case might well have voted down the proposal simply
because it did not firmly bind the states to the Bill of Rights,[76]
something which was probably viewed as the principal constitutional
need at the time.

But Garfield's point was still well taken. Whatever the Radicals may have had in mind, it is also clear that some members voted
against the amendment because they felt it gave Congress plenary
power; they feared total centralization and complete elimination
of states rights.[77] This means that the full implications of the
natural rights theory cannot be accepted. It seems reasonably
clear that an amendment which could result in complete centralization in the federal government of what is generally known as "police
power" was not acceptable to two-thirds of the Congress.

Inadequacy of Defense of the Traditional View of Congressional Enforcement Power

On the other hand, the heart of the natural rights theory
argument remains, and it certainly does not follow that the traditional Supreme Court view of the Fourteenth Amendment's meaning
permitting no congressional authority to enforce against private
action is correct. That traditional view has been defended by
Alfred Avins,[78] but his case is not convincing. His work stresses
the difference between the two Bingham proposals. But he ignores
the likelihood that the stress on restricting the states in the
second proposal stems not from a state action-private action distinction but results from the Radical belief that this emphasis
would cure the major existing constitutional deficiency. As previously discussed, the Radicals had reason to believe that rights
recognized in the Constitution were automatically enforceable
against private individuals. And the record does seem clear that
opposition to Bingham's first proposal among those who feared
over-centralization was not to congressional power over private
action <u>per se</u>, but to direct and plenary congressional power to
punish deprivations of basic rights. Avins' citing of Bingham to
the effect that Bingham wished no change in the Constitution ignores the fact that Bingham's view of what was already in the
Constitution was rather unique. Other Bingham quotes presented
are also a bit deceptive. Bingham's assertion that the Congress
could not pass penal legislation was made in regard to the Civil
Rights Bill of 1866 <u>before</u> the Fourteenth Amendment was passed.
His strong statements about his objective of binding the states
and their officers reflects his belief in the importance of that
objective; it does not prove he felt that private action could
not be reached.

Avins is aware of the influence upon the framers of the doctrine of Prigg v. Pennsylvania.[79] He attempts to circumvent the
problem which Prigg presents to the traditional view by asserting
that Bingham's first constitutional proposal was an embodiment of
the Prigg rule and thus, that the rejection of this proposal also
constituted a rejected by Congress of the Prigg rule. But this
is a rather arbitrary interpretation. If anything, the absence
of wording in the second draft empowering Congress clearly to reach
private action most plausible indicated a reliance on the Prigg
rule, not its repudiation.

The evidence of Congressional intent does not permit Avins to
sustain the traditional judicial view of Congress' Fourteenth Amendment enforcement power as limited exclusively to state action and
at that, to punishment of state officials who willfully deny protection. Thus, the movement by the Supreme Court in recent years away
from this narrow view does not break faith with the framers. But,
as already discussed, the full implications of the natural rights theory
cannot be accepted either. The second draft of Bingham's proposal
did differ from the first. There is reason to think that the revi-
sion did stem at least in part from the need to pacify those who
were opposed to granting Congress the direct, plenary power to
legislate regarding all of the traditional rights to life, liberty
and property, and whose support was needed to obtain the two-thirds
vote required for passage.

The Inadequacy of the Intermediate "Remedial" Theory

The only major study that takes an intermediate position on
the matter is Harris' The Quest for Equality.[80] Harris believes
that during this period the Congress was essentially divided into
three groups: the Radicals who stood for the natural rights theory
and all its implications; the conservatives who opposed the whole
concept and who later brought forward the idea that the Fourteenth
Amendment simply provided for the over-ruling of improper acts of
state governemnts; and the moderates who stood between the other
groups.[81]

The moderates essentially accepted the natural rights theory,
but were uneasy about the threat it posed to federalism. Harris
explains their position on the basis of statements made during the
debates over the enforcement acts of the 1870's and he feels their
position is basically valid. He believes they were willing to sanc-
tion the exercise by Congress of enforcement power over both private
and state deprivations of rights, but only remedially,[82] that is,
after the states had failed to protect the rights.

This analysis has value as far as it goes. But at the center of Harris' position lies the crucial and unanswered question: who determines when a state has failed in its duty? It cannot be that the moderates of the Reconstruction Congress were simply arguing that the Congress itself would first have to make some sort of official determination that the states had failed in their Four-teenth Amendment duties before it could act, for this pro forma device standing alone would make meaningless their vigorous protes-tations against Congress' having plenary power over the rights of citizens.

On the other hand, if they envisioned some sort of meaningful check on Congress by requiring the reality of state failure to be submitted to judicial determination, they would be advocating a course to which the Radicals surely could not have agreed. Putting control over the effective exercise of Congress' power in the hands of the judiciary is something which the Radicals, with their well-known political hostility to the courts, would never have counten-anced.[83] Certainly, at very least this is true insofar as the exer-cise of this enforcement power was seen as necessary to protect Negroes and northerners in the southern states.

The two-thirds majority that passed the Amendment surely did consist of both Radicals and moderates. And although the reasons for rejection of Bingham's first proposal were probably multiple, it does seem that those who feared for the federal system did re-quire some pacification. Therefore, Harris' description of the moderates' general view of the proper scope of Congress' enforce-ment power is probably valid.

But Harris' work seems to imply that the moderates' interpre-tation should be accepted as the best expression of the original intent. This would be valid if the view of the moderates was simply a dilution of the Radical position, for the Radicals would then have presumably agreed that the Amendment for which they were voting did at least what the moderates claimed for it. But since there appears to have been a basic contradiction between the moderates' concept of remedial power and the Radical position, Radical acquies-cence in the moderate view certainly cannot be assumed.

Conclusion: No Common Ground

Both factions voted for the Amendment, Radicals believing that it still enacted the entire natural rights theory, moderates believ-ing that it expressed a limitation of Congress' enforcement role to a genuinely remedial one.[84] But it does seem that no satisfactory theoretical common denominator between the intent of the Radicals and that of the moderates existed at the time of the framing and enactment. That is why no single view of the original intent as to Congress' power to enforce the fourteenth amendment has gained general acceptance. There was no single original view which can plausibly be advanced as having the support of two-thirds of the members of both houses and utilized to fully legitimate Supreme Court interpretation of Congress' Fourteenth Amendment enforcement power today.

Constitutional majorities of two-thirds are, of course, larger than is normally required in legislative affairs. But experience and common sense tells us that the kind of situation that prevailed here is likely to exist in many other situations where courts find that the plain words of a statute do not yield clarity. Of course there may be times when the original legislative intent will spring out at the searcher, the ambiguity in the statute being a simple matter of bad draftsmanship. But it may well be that a matter is ambiguous just because of fundamental disagreement at the time of passage.

Concern over judicial restraint growing out of the experience of the first three decades of this century and the resultant thrust toward deference to legislatures have led many legal commentators to an easy but simplistic acceptance of the degree to which legislatures operate in accordance with the assumptions of classical democratic theory. As Martin Shapiro has pointed out,[85] it is a highly debatable piece of conventional wisdom that portrays elected legislatures and executives as the unvarying exponents of "the majority view." Close observers of legislatures in particular recognize that in many situations there is no majority view; there may only be two or perhaps several minority interests in contention. Thus the frequent objective of individual legislators is not to respond to (or oppose) "majority" sentiment; it is to accommodate the pressure to act on an issue while antagonizing as few of the competing minority interests as possible. One of the most common legislative responses to such a situation is the enactment of "strategically vague" legislation which each minority interest will hopefully construe as meeting its needs or satisfying its objections. Clarification is a future burden to be assumed by some subsequent legislature, or the administrative agency charged with the legislation's implementation, or perhaps ultimately, the courts. While such legislative behavior may appear irresponsible to some, it is a political fact of life which courts, among others, will inevitably have to face.

Admittedly, reasonable men may differ on the question of just how judges should go about the business of construing ambiguous legislative products in the absence of a clear legislative intent. But the efforts to construct appropriate and legitimate rationales and mechanisms for such judicial discretion will not be aided by refusing to face the issue through continuing efforts which obscure the bounds between legal history and legal fiction. Had the effort to return to the 1860's and 1870's described herein been undertaken for the limited purpose of demonstrating that much of the Supreme Court's own interpretation of the Fourteenth Amendment during the late 1800's was a clear distortion of the original lines of legal development, thus undercutting its value as precedent, then it would have been justified. But pressing beyond that point in a search for a literal intent goes too far.

It is one thing for the Supreme Court to search out the roots to help clear away the doctrinal weeds which stemmed from reaction and racism, and choked off much of the original plant. But the Court itself must accept the responsibility for the growth and evolution of Fourteenth Amendment doctrine in response to changing circumstances over a period of 110 years. It cannot and should not look to the Congress of the 1860's for a detailed blueprint designed to serve for all time to come.

SECTION II - References

1. Alexander Bickel, The Supreme Court and the Idea of Progress, (New York: Harper and Row, 1970), p. 13, from a phrase of L.B. Namier's.

2. See for example, Brown v. Board of Education, 347 U.S. 483 (1954); Katzenbach v. Morgan, 384, U.S. 641, (1966); South Carolina v. Katzenbach, 383 U.S. 301, (1966); Jones v. Mayer, 392, U.S. 409 (1968): U.S. v. Guest, 383 U.S. 745 (1966).

3. 18 USCA§ 241, 18 USCA§ 242, 42 USCA§ 1983, 42 USCA§ 1985 (3), 42 USCA§ 1981, 42 USCA§ 1982, which are derived, respectively, from the Civil Rights Act of 1870, 16 Stat. 140; the Civil Rights Act of 1866, 35 Stat. 1092; the Ku Klux Act of 1871, 17 Stat. 13; again the Ku Klux Act of 1871, 17 Stat. 13; and the last two again from the Civil Rights Act of 1866, 35 Stat. 1092.

4. See for example, Monroe v. Pape, 365 U.S. 167, 81 S.Ct. 475, (1961) U.S. v. Guest 383 U.S. 745, 86 S.Ct. 1170 (1966); Jones v. Mayer, 392 U.S. 409, 38 S.Ct. 2186 (1968); Griffen v. Breckenridge, 403 U.S. 88; 91 S.Ct. 1795 (1971).

5. Section 5 reads: "The Congress shall have power to enforce this article by appropriate legislation." Section 1 reads: "All persons born or naturalized in the United States and subject to the jurisdiction thereof, are citizens of the United States and of the State wherein they reside. No State shall make or enforce any law which shall abridge the privileges or immunities of citizens of the United States; nor shall any State deprive any person of life, liberty or property, without due process of law; nor deny to any person the equal protection of the laws.

6. 109 U.S. 3 (1883).

7. 383 U.S. 745 (1966).

8. 109 U.S. 3, 11-12 (1883).

9. Archibald Cox, "Foreword: Constitutional Adjudication and the Promotion of Human Rights," Harvard Law Review, Vol. 80, (1966) p. 91.

10. 14 Stat. 27, Sec. 1, Be it enacted by the Senate and House of Representatives of the United States of America in Congress assembled, that all persons born in the United States and not

subject to any foreign power, excluding Indians not taxed, are hereby declared to be citizens of the United States; and such citizens, of every race and color, without regard to any previous condition of slavery or involuntary servitude, except as a punishment for crime whereof the party shall have been duly convicted, shall have the same right, in every State and Territory in the United States, to make and enforce contracts, to sue, be parties, and give evidence, to inherit, purchase, lease, sell, hold, and convey real and personal property, and to full and equal benefit of all laws and proceedings for the security of person and property, as is enjoyed by white citizens, and shall be subject to like punishment, pains, and penalties, and to none other, any law, statute, ordinance, regulation, or custom, to the contrary notwithstanding.

Section 2, And be it further enacted, that any person who, under color of law, statute, ordinance, regulation, or custom, shall subject, or cause to be subjected, any inhabitant of any State or Territory to the deprivation of any right secured or protected by this act, or to different punishment, pains, or penalties on account of such person having at any time been held in a condition of slavery or involuntary servitude, except as a punishment for crime whereof the party shall have been duly convicted, or by reason of his color or race, than is prescribed for the punishment of white persons, shall be deemed guilty of a misdemeanor, and, or imprisonment not exceeding one year, or both, in the discretion of the court.

11. Amendment XIII. Section 1, Neither slavery nor involuntary servitude, except as punishment for crime whereof the party shall have been duly convicted, shall exist within the United States or any place subject to their jurisdiction.

     Section 2, Congress shall have power to enforce this article by appropriate legislation.

12. Congressional Globe, 39th Congress, 1st Session, pp. 1290-1293 (1865). This session's Globe will henceforth be cited as 39 Globe.

13. 39 Globe, pp. 474-475.

14. 39 Globe, p. 1366.

15. 39 Globe, p. 1367.

16. <u>39 Globe</u>, p. 1861.

17. Alex. Bickel, "The Original Understanding and the Segregation
    Decision," <u>Harvard Law Review</u>, Vol. 69 (1955), p. 1, re-
    printed in <u>Selected Essays in Constitutional Law</u>, (St. Paul:
    West Publishing Co., 1963), p. 872, footnote 61.

18. Benj. B. Kendrick, <u>The Journal of the Joint Committee of
    Fifteen on Reconstruction, 39th Congress 1865-1867</u>, (Columbia
    University Studies in History, Economics, and Public Law,
    Vol. LXII, New York: Columbia University Press, 1914), p.
    41; Introduced earlier in Congress, see <u>39 Globe</u>, p. 10.

19. <u>Ibid</u>, p. 46.

20. <u>Ibid</u>.

21. <u>Ibid</u>, pp. 60-61.

22. <u>39 Globe</u>, pp. 1033-1035.

23. <u>39 Globe</u>, p. 1095.

24. Kendrick, <u>Journal</u>, p. 85.

25. <u>Ibid</u>, p. 87.

26. <u>Ibid</u>, p. 98.

27. <u>Ibid</u>, p. 99.

28. <u>Ibid</u>, pp. 101-102.

29. <u>Ibid</u>, p. 106.

30. 19 Howard (U.S.) 393 (1857).

31. James, <u>Framing</u>, p. 179, TenBroek, <u>Equal Under Law</u>, p. 201,
    Flack, <u>Adoption</u>, pp. 94-95, Harris, <u>Search</u>, pp. 34-35, Bickel,
    "Original Understanding," <u>Selected Essays in Constitutional
    Law</u>, pp. 853-892.

32. Mark DeWolfe Howe, "Federalism and Civil Rights," in <u>Civil
    Rights, The Constitution and the Courts</u>, (Cambridge: Harvard
    University Press, 1967), p. 47, John Roche, <u>Courts and Rights</u>,
    (New York: Random House, 1966), p. 72, TenBroek, <u>Equal</u>,

p. 180 argues that the 1866 Civil Rights Bill's "full and equal benefit of all laws and proceedings for the security of persons and property," (first section) implies protection against private acts and therefore the second section must have logically been intended to do so. He cites the reports of General Grant and Carl Schurz to Congress pointing out that they agree on the need to protect newly freed Negroes from private persecution as well as state sponsored injustices.

It should also be noted that in recent years the Supreme Court has held that the Bill's first section does reach private action under Thirteenth Amendment authority. Jones v. Mayer, 392 U.S. 409 (1968). But the Court has not held that the penal or enforcement section being discussed here (section two) is applicable to private action.

33. S. 60. See 39 Globe, pp. 129-209; Presidential veto not over-ridden in the Senate. The Freedman's Bureau was created by the Act of March 3, 1865, 13 Stat. 507.

34. (Baltimore: Johns Hopkins Press, 1908.)

35. Congressional Globe, 42nd Congress, 1st Session, Appendix (1872), pp. 83-85. (Hereafter cited as 42 Appendix.)

36. The Bill passed and was re-passed by 2/3 vote over a presidential veto. Bingham was one of only six Republicans to oppose its passage.

37. Flack devoted a chapter (IV) to examining expressions of opinion in state legislatures when the proposed amendment came before them. However, these legislatures could not alter what was submitted and any reservations or qualifications that were expressed are, of course, in no way binding. In fact, they offer rather little in the way of clues to congressional intent because of their physical and temporal distance from Congress and the process of actually shaping the Amendment.

38. There is, of course, an entire literature concerning the alleged conspiracy to place corporations under the due process guarantee provided for "persons"; the theory was developed by the Beards in The Rise of American Civilization and based upon Roscoe Conkling's testimony in Santa Clara v. Southern Pacific Railway, 11 U.S. 394 (1886). It was refuted in Graham, "The Conspiracy Theory of the Fourteenth Amendment," Yale Law Journal Vol. 47 (1938), p. 371 and Yale Law Journal, Vol. 48 (1938), p. 171.

39. *42 Appendix*, pp. 83-85, particularly: "These eight Articles
     [the first eight amendments to the Constitution] I have shown
     never were limitations upon the power of the States, until
     made so by the Fourteenth Amendment. The words of that Amend-
     ment, 'no State shall make or enforce any law which shall
     abridge the privileges or immunities of citizens of the United
     States', are an express prohibition upon every State of the
     Union, which may be enforced under existing laws of Congress
     and such other laws for their better enforcement as Congress
     may make."

40. *Equal Under Law* (originally entitled, *The Anti-Slavery Origins
     of the Fourteenth Amendment*) (New York: Collier Books, 1965).

41. *Report of the Joint Committee on Reconstruction*, 39th Congress
     1st Session (1865). The Report presents many instances of
     private violence: attempts being made to disarm Negroes by
     patrols; roving combinations of citizens (p. 127); a young
     girl beaten, bare, by her former master (p. 170); four young
     men riding around, armed, finding a Negro owned previously by
     the father of one of them, beating him, and then leaving him
     to die (p. 184). On p. 208, Lt. Col. Clap describes an in-
     stance where several returned rebel soldiers went into a town
     shooting and beating Union men. On their return they came
     across a Negro on a public highway and castrated and murdered
     him. No effort was made to arrest them, and they continued
     their outrages against Negroes. Clap then says of the thou-
     sands of cases of murder, robbery, and maltreatment of freed-
     men and Union citizens he has heard of, he knows of no case
     where the local authorities made any effort to apprehend any
     of the offenders.

     Reports of organized violence directed against Negroes were
     featured in the northern press. There were also riots in the
     South, regarded by some as the last straw. Such alterations
     caused great revulsion in the northern states. John Hope
     Franklin, *Reconstruction after the Civil War* (Chicago: Uni-
     versity of Chicago Press, 1961) pp. 51-64.

42. TenBroek, *Equal*, pp. 94-131, 235.

43. H. Graham, "Our 'Declaratory' Fourteenth Amendment," *Stanford
     Law Review*, Vol. 7 (1954), p. 3.

44. "The definition of citizenship contained in the first clause
     was generally regarded as declaratory of what was law. Some
     thought the only need for such clarification arose from Taney's

decision in the <u>Dred Scott Case</u>." James, <u>Framing</u>, pp. 179-180.

45. 16 Wall, 36 (1873).

46. Even if one is not personally convinced by natural rights theory, it is clear that the political foundation of our Republic rests upon it -- consider the Declaration of Independence -- and so does our constitutional law. See <u>The "Higher Law" Background of American Constitutional Law</u> by Edward Corwin (Ithaca: Cornell University Press, 1955).

47. <u>U.S. v. Wheeler</u>, 254 U.S. 281 (1920) might be considered an exception. However, that case's authority has been considerably eroded. In <u>U.S. v. Guest</u>, 383 U.S. 741, note 16 (1966), the Court said: "Whatever continuing validity <u>Wheeler</u> may have as restricted to its own facts, the dicta in the <u>Wheeler</u> opinion relied on by the District Court in the present case have been discredited in subsequent decisions. Cf, <u>Edwards v. .... California</u>, 314 U.S. 160, 177 ... (Douglas, J., concurring); <u>U.S. v. Williams</u>, 341 U.S. 70, 80 ..."

48. See Bickel, "Original Understanding..."; note also Justice Bradley's language in the <u>Civil Rights Cases</u>. There is a strong suggestion that he views the privileges and immunities of U.S. citizens as encompassing the traditional rights of life, liberty, and property but is unwilling to see them extended to "social rights" such as the right to be served in a privately owned restaurant without regard to race, 109 U.S. 3, 24-25 (1883).

49. TenBroek, <u>Equal</u>, p. 205.

The summary of the evidence presented earlier in this study deliberately refrains from extracting just the civil rights proposals as TenBroek does.

50. J. James, <u>The Framing of the Fourteenth Amendment</u>, (Urbana: University of Illinois Press 1956).

51. James, <u>The Framing of the Fourteenth Amendment</u>: Harris, <u>The Search for Equality</u>, p. 35.

52. In April of 1886, Bingham was reported, by Robert Owen, who claims to have heard it from Stevens, to have still believed that Congress should spell out in detail the "civil rights"

that were being guaranteed. Owen, "Political Results from the Varioloid," 35 Atlantic Monthly, pp. 660, 662-664, (1875), cited in Bickel, "Original Understanding..." in Selected Essays, p. 880.

53. Conferral of suffrage was finally abandoned in 1866 in response to an increasingly widespread belief among Republicans that it would be a potentially disastrous political move at that time, according to James, Framing, p. 180, and Flack, Adoption, p. 70. Bingham's ultimate triumph in the midst of a tendency to caution suggests he may have finally succeeded by repeating the sort of argument he had made about the language of the original Civil Rights Act of 1866. For most Congressmen, the most important effect of including section one in the Fourteenth Amendment was to write the Civil Rights Act of 1866 into the Constitution. This put the Act beyond repeal by any renewed Democratic majority. Even those Congressmen who opposed the Amendment and the Act saw matters this way. (For example, Eldridge, 39 Globe, p. 2506.)

54. Bingham's original affirmative amendment was rejected and the comments of its opponents indicate opposition to giving Congress plenary power. The language was changed to its present negative phrasing and reassurances were given that the section contained nothing new. Of course, to a moderate "nothing new" doubtless meant that the proposed amendment worked no revolution in jurisdiction over enforcing basic rights; to the Radicals it was "nothing new" because this statement of the "natural rights" position was already in the Constitution, the Supreme Court to the contrary notwithstanding. See Graham, "Our 'Declaratory' Fourteenth Amendment," Stanford Law Review, Vol. 7 (1954), p. 3.

55. 42 Appendix, pp. 150-154.

56. R. J. Harris, The Quest for Equality (Baton Rouge: Louisiana State University Press, 1960), p. 34; see also reference in Freund, Sutherland, Howe, Brown, Constitutional Law, (Boston: Little Brown, 1961), p. 881.

57. 42 Appendix, pp. 83-85.

58. 39 Globe, p. 1034.

59. 3 U.S. 243 (1833), In this case, the Supreme Court held that the prohibitions against governmental interference with basic

rights contained in the first ten amendments to the national
Constitution applied to the federal government only, and not
to the state governments.

60. James, Framing, p. 190.

61. 24 How. 66 (1861).

62. 16 Peters 539 (1842).

63. The Constitution of the United States.

64. Mark DeWolfe Howe, "Federalism and Civil Rights," in Cox,
    Howe and Wiggins, Civil Rights, The Constitution and the
    Courts, (Cambridge: Harvard University Press, 1967), p. 43.

65. 24 How. 66 (1861).

66. 24 How. 66, 107-110 (1861).

67. 16 Peters 539, 615 (1842).

68. "If constitutional law had terminated with Prigg v. Pennsyl-
    vania, scholars and lawyers could confidently assert that
    there is nothing in the nature of American federalism that
    disables the Congress from controlling private conduct affect-
    the civil rights of others." Howe, "Federalism...", p. 45.
    One might add that if constitutional law had terminated with
    Kentucky v. Dennison and Barron v. Baltimore, one could assert
    that there was also nothing that would enable the Congress to
    control state action affecting civil rights.

69. 39 Globe, p. 1034.

70. 39 Globe, pp. 1064-1065, 1088-1094.

71. Congress shall have power to make all laws which shall be neces-
    sary and proper to secure to the citizens of each state all
    privileges and immunities of citizens in the several States
    (Art. 4, Sect. 2); and to all persons in the several States
    equal protection in the rights of life, liberty and property
    (5th Amendment). Kendrick, Journal, pp. 60, 61.

72. Expressed in dispute over the Enforcement Act of 1871,
    42 Appendix, pp. 83-85.

73. <u>39 Globe</u>, pp. 1063-1965.

74. Bickel, "Original Understanding ...," p. 891.

75. James, Framing, p. 86.

76. As to what exactly was meant by "The Bill of Rights," see Charles Fairman, "Does the Fourteenth Amendment Incorporate the Bill of Rights? The Original Understanding," <u>Stanford Law Review</u>, Vol. 5 (1949), p. 5.

77. James, <u>Framing</u>, p. 87; <u>39 Globe</u>, pp. 1059-1066, 1085-1987.

78. Alfred Avins, "Federal Power to Punish Individual Crimes Under the Fourteenth Amendment: The Original Understanding," Memorandum in <u>Civil Rights</u>, Hearings before the Subcommittee on the Judiciary, U.S. Senate, 89th Congress, 2nd Session (1966), p. 754.

79. 16 Peters 539 (1842).

80. (Baton Rouge: Louisiana State Press, 1960), Harris' thinking was further developed by Laurant Frantz in his study, "Congressional Power to Enforce the Fourteenth Amendment Against Private Action," <u>Yale Law Journal</u>, Vol. 73 (1964) p. 1352.

81. Harris, <u>Search</u>, p. 45.

82. The term remedial as applied to the Fourteenth Amendment enforcement has been used in different ways at different times. Some have utilized it to mean that Congress cannot pass legislation "prophylactically" by making certain courses of conduct by state officers illegal in advance of an actual offense to the Amendment; Congress's power is then described as remedial, meaning that it is limited exclusively to the undoing of improper state action after it has taken place.

    As Harris uses the term, however, remedial power is distinguished from plenary power over the basic rights of free men. Thus Congress may enact laws in advance of any offense, and these laws may reach both state and private action, but the laws are to be used in a supplementary manner to remedy deficiencies in an obligation that remains primarily with the states.

83. "(T)he Radicals did not trust the judiciary in general and the Supreme Court in particular, either before or after the

passage of the resolution submitting the proposed amendment
to the states. Former Abolitionists had not forgiven the
Court for its decision in the Dred Scott case or for ...
Taney's circuit court opinion in Ex Parte Merryman. 17 Fed.
Cas. No. 9487 (1861). "The hostility of Radicals to the Court
was intensified by Chief Justice Salmon P. Chase's refusal
to hold circuit court in states under martial law, thereby
preventing the trial of Jefferson Davis, and the fears that
their reconstruction policies would be invalidated," Harris,
Search, pp. 53-54. And of course, the Abolitionist position
had not fared well in adjudication of the Fugitive Slave Laws.
See also James, Framing, p. 184.

Now B. Kutler in Judicial Power and Reconstruction Politics
(Chicago: University of Chicago Press, 1968), pp. 21-22,
states that Republicans were optimistic about the Court in
1865 and early 1866 because of Chief Justice Chase's clear
commitment to the anti-slavery cause and the fact that a
clear majority of Justices had been appointed by Lincoln.
He feels that "the Republicans respected the Court as an
institution, recognized a place and function for it in the
scheme of government and seemed confident of the kind of role
it would play." But in light of the history of the Abolitionists, the Dred Scott decision, and the sharp distinctiveness
of the Radical constitutional theories, Kutler's description
seems rather overstated. Of course, the Republicans may well
have been hopeful about the role of the Court in the future.
But that is really beside the point.

The point being made here is that in light of the very aggres-
sive behavior shown by the Radicals all through the war in
regard to presidential power, their creation of a special congressional directorate on Reconstruction matters (the Joint
Committee), their audacious passage of the Civil Rights Bill
of 1866 on the questionable authority of the Thirteenth
Amendment, and their cavalier treatment of the Supreme Court
in the months to follow, it is scarcely likely that these men,
who believed very strongly in the natural rights theory, would
have stood still for the notion that the Congressional enforcement power they wrote into this very important Amendment could
not go into effect until there had been a judicial determination that a state was deficient or delinquent in its Fourteenth
Amendment duty.

84. The issue of independent judicial evaluation of the reality of state failure as precondition to congressional exercise of remedial authority under the Reconstruction amendments remains alive. In Katzenbach v. Morgan, 384, U.S. 641 (1966) the majority was willing to let Congress itself decide that no person who had successfully completed the sixth grade in an accredited Puerto Rican school where instruction did not take place in English could be denied the vote due to a failure to pass a literacy test. This had the effect of nullifying New York's English literacy requirement, enfranchising about a quarter of a million Puerto Ricans resident in New York City. In a vigorous dissent, Justice Harlan, joined by Justice Stewart, argued that Congress must first establish to the Court's satisfaction that there has been a violation of a state's constitutional obligations before Congress can apply remedial legislation.

85. Martin Shapiro, Freedom of Speech: The Supreme Court and Judicial Review, (Englewood Cliffs: Prentice Hall, 1966).

SECTION III

FOURTEENTH AMENDMENT LIBERTIES
FROM A PLURALIST PERSPECTIVE

One of the more provocative constitutional problems of the
1960's remains unsettled. It involves the tension between the
objectives of maintaining the essential balance of the federal
system and that of providing the Congress with sufficient power
to protect the basic rights of minorities from private attack
when state authorities fail to protect them. In a 1966 article,[1]
Professor Archibald Cox argued that Supreme Court decisions in
South Carolina v. Katzenbach[2] and Katzenbach v. Morgan,[3] when com-
bined with the dicta of a majority of the justices in U.S. v.
Guest,[4] provided a firm basis for the conclusion that the congressional legislative power could now reach private action in attempting to secure Fourteenth Amendment rights.[5] Perhaps his most con-
troversial contention was that there was no convincing way of
distinguishing "equal protection rights" from "due process rights."[6]
Echoing Justice Bradley in the Civil Rights Cases,[7] Cox was of
the opinion that Congress, if it desired, now also had the power
to prevent states from denying life, liberty and property without
due process of law by enacting a superseding federal code of municipal conduct which would effectively displace the states from
their traditional police power activities, destroying the essence
of the federal system.[8] In other words, this "new" constitutional
interpretation which approved congressional power to protect the
basic rights of minorities from private attack seemed inevitably
to require approval of congressional power to protect the basic
rights of every American from such attack.

Cox was not concerned that, although Congress had this power,
they would soon exercise it.[9] But it is not unreasonable to think
that concern over the possible consequences of explicitly further
expanding Congress' Fourteenth Amendment enforcement authority led
the Court in the late 1960's to the politically more conservative,
and legally rather sudden resuscitation of the Thirteenth Amendment as a source of power for congressional action to eliminate
private discrimination against Blacks as a badge of slavery;[10] it
is much less likely that the Thirteenth Amendment can be expanded
to threaten all state power. But is it wise to read into the
Constitution what amounts, as a practical matter, to a total grant
of power to Congress to act to protect the rights of Black Americans from private deprivation, while powers of such scope are not
available to protect any other segment of the population?[11]

Despite its current priority,[12] racial discrimination is not
the only civil rights problem America faces now or may face in the
future. Is there no plausible way in which the more comprehensive
Fourteenth Amendment may be used to protect all Americans from un-
fair discrimination, public and private, without conceding to the
Congress the constitutional authority to supersede state police

power across the board? I suggest that there is, but that the
obstacle to perceiving it has been the traditional "individualist"
perspective on civil liberties. This perspective, when applied
to this problem, sees only a political conflict between two levels
of government as to which shall bear the primary authority and
responsibility for vindicating the rights and liberties of the
individual American. I suggest that if a pluralist perspective
on civil liberties is utilized in this situation, it offers valu-
able insight into the political and social functions of developing
Fourteenth Amendment doctrine and a resolution of the dilemma of
Fourteenth Amendment enforcement.

The Pluralist Perspective

Civil liberties conflicts, including those related to the
Fourteenth Amendment, are conventionally depicted as struggles
between the government and an individual, State v. John Doe. This
is, of course, a valid perspective, but it has tended to over-
shadow an equally important one. The development of civil liberties has always been closely, perhaps primarily, connected with
group conflicts. In Democracy in the U.S.[13] William Riker stresses
the close historical and functional relationship between "faction"
and civil liberties.

> Responsible popular government requires ... the
> clarifying hand of faction. Factions, organized
> into political parties, define issues and ideolo-
> gies for elections by means of their incessant
> controversy.[14]

Riker quotes Madison in Federalist 10, "Liberty is to faction what
air is to fire"; then he continues:

> A national atmosphere of the traditional democratic
> liberties is indeed the only condition in which
> faction will blaze up. In our own day the ideals
> of the eighteenth century bills of rights have be-
> come ends-in-themselves. Freedom of religion and
> expression, fair criminal procedures and the like
> seem now to be no small part of the self-direction
> and self-respect we hope democracy can give us. We
> often forget therefore, that they have an institu-
> tional significance also. Their original purpose
> was, in fact, not so much to dignify mankind as to
> foster faction and distribute dissent.[15]

It is widely understood that the historical origins of our
major guarantees of civil liberty are rooted in factional conflict;
that religious liberty was fashioned by and, in turn supports,
"the oldest kind of factionalism in Western Europe,"[16] and that
most of the great Anglo-American procedural protections grew out
of factional struggles between the English kings and their opponents.[17] Nevertheless, perhaps because of our American individualist philosophical tradition, when civil liberties are considered
as a subject for current study, they are usually depicted by
scholars as, what Riker calls, "a part of the democratic ideal of
self-respect" and "self-direction."[18] Little recognition is given
to the fact that they are "all of a method"[19] -- that the "institutional significance"[20] of civil liberties in democratic governments is not the elevation of status of the individual, it is the
encouragement of factions. Thus civil liberties may well be defined
as the institutional political arrangements that permit citizens
who wish to defend, pursue or promote varied cultural, economic or
political interests freely, openly and peacefully to coalesce,
organize and interact towards their respective ends.

Accordingly, the development of civil liberties as both cause
and effect of factional conflict is not limited historically to
the English revolutionary period. The close relationship between
civil liberties and factional conflict has continued down to the
present day in our own country. Indeed the great nationalizing
civil liberties revolution that has been brought about by the
Fourteenth Amendment over the last century has been intimately
related to factional or group conflicts. Although frequently described as a process of making the guarantees of individual liberty
contained in the Bill of Rights selectively binding upon the states,
the development of the Fourteenth Amendment guarantees should also
be described in terms of group or factional political conflicts
and the changing pattern of American social and political pluralism.

Nevertheless, such legal developments are still analyzed almost exclusively in terms of individuals and their rights.[21] The
Fourteenth Amendment is usually seen as a vehicle for imposing
upon the states the great protections of individual liberties
contained in the Bill of Rights, thus making the individual's freedom more secure by establishing national constitutional restraints
applying to all levels of government.[22]

Of course, most commentators would probably agree that the use
of the Equal Protection Clause to destroy the racial caste system
in this country might be most aptly described not as an extension
of freedom for individuals but as the liberation of an entire class
of persons; equal protection litigation has been traditionally concerned almost exclusively with claims of improper legislative

- 67 -

classification. But few seem to recognize that almost all major
Fourteenth Amendment decisions, including those decided on grounds
of due process rather than equal protection, are fundamentally
concerned with matters of group or class rights and not just individual rights.

The picture of due process litigation that is usually put
forward in most the literature is one of the Supreme Court imposing or reiterating a general definition of a civil liberty, and
thus vindicating an individual plaintiff who had put forward a
claim to some fundamental freedom which a state had failed to
recognize.[23] But the fact is that most states do recognize virtually all of the major freedoms specified in the national Bill
of Rights and have done so since well before the Court began the
process of incorporation.[24] In the typical case the Supreme Court
is actually faced with a situation where the state action amounts
to an explicit or implicit refusal to extend the guaranteed freedoms to one segment of its population. This is not to deny the
validity of the traditional view that the Supreme Court is engaged
in a process of defining the substantive qualities of a given freedom, its nature and boundaries. Nevertheless, the practical circumstances surrounding virtually all major instances of Supreme
Court adjudication of the substantive aspects of prominent constitutional rights have not reflected a state acting to eliminate an
entire freedom, to prohibit as criminal and anti-social the total
exercise of some generally valued liberty. Rather, such cases
have usually involved claims by or on behalf of a segment of the
population to the effect that the established substantive definition of the freedom in question was such as to improperly exclude
them from its scope of protection.

The groups pressing substantive claims are usually readily
identifiable, particularly in "first amendment" cases involving
religion or political free speech.[25] And although procedural
rights may be seen as more closely tied to peculiar individual
circumstances, it remains apparent that the great expansion of
procedural rights during the past two decades has been closely
tied to an equalitarian effort to provide meaningful protection
for racial minorities, the poor and other disadvantaged groups.[26]

In a policy with a significant amount of popular participation, laws that really do deny all or most of the population some
important freedom will not normally be enacted. Thus civil liberties questions usually arise when society stigmatizes as criminal,
or at least fails to recognize as worthy or respectable, the
valued activities or proclivities of a segment of the population.
The Supreme Court is then called upon the "rescue" the segment.
True, litigation involving incorporated due process rights is
usually pleaded on the formal ground that the incorporated Bill

- 68 -

of Rights article in question requires the state to leave the individual plaintiff alone. But in reality, the Court is usually being
asked to extend the definition of a given freedom to cover the
needs of a particular class of people and to determine that they
should not be excluded because they constitute a legitimate if
peculiar social grouping, and are not merely representative individual examples of anti-social behavior capable of general and
more or less random manifestation.

The distinction between those individuals whose behavior has
been of a sort properly prohibited and those whose behavior should
be permitted as incident to membership in a legitimate political
or cultural grouping is, obviously, not always easily made. Nevertheless it is the underlying issue in most major Fourteenth Amendment controversies: the legitimacy of a claim of a segment of
society to the equal exercise of basic liberties. Indeed most
due process civil liberties decisions of the Supreme Court could
probably have been based upon the Equal Protection Clause had the
Due Process Clause not existed, although as a technical matter,
the argument would probably have been more difficult to make.

The Fourteenth Amendment and the Pattern of Pluralism

While group analysis is not new to the political study of
constitutional law, most efforts have been limited to pointing
out the relation between the efforts of certain organized groups
and the ultimate adjudication of specific cases in which they had
an interest.[27] But some insight into the change in the overall
pattern of relationships among politically significant groupings
that has been reflected in and supported by envolving Fourteenth
Amendment doctrine can be found in existing literature.

Of course, the century which has seen the development of
Fourteenth Amendment civil liberties doctrine has been a period
of major social change in America, a time of urbanization and
industrialization with the decline of the old, rural small-town
America and the rise of a modern, cosmopolitan, urban and subur-
ban nation. Writing of the earlier America, John Roche observed
that it was not the "golden age" of freedom which some like to
believe.[28] He claims that whatever diversity of opinion existed

> was a consequence not of tolerance and mutual
> respect ... but of the existence of many com-
> munities within the society, each with its own
> canons of orthodoxy. In other words, if one
> looked hard enough, it was probable that he
> would find somewhere in the U.S. a community
> that shared his own peculiar views -- whether

religious, vegetarian, polygamous, Socialist, or
whatever -- and joining it, he could help imposing
group beliefs on all within reach.

In short, one could find a microcosm to be intolerant with, and the U.S. was notoriously the happy
hunting ground of what Reisman has acutely termed
"vested heresies." True there was no centralized
authoritarian state on the European model...but...
the centralized state is not the only institution
capable of oppression; the parish can be as severe
in its impact on the individual as the centralized
variety.[29]

According to this view, the U.S. in the last century was not an
integrated national community but "a number of subcultures liv-
ing side by side within the geographical expanse of the nation."[30]
Andrew Hacker says that "the majority of Americans spent their
lives in circumscribed settings which, if not literally feudal,
nevertheless forced regimens that tolerated little deviation from
established local standards."[31] Freedom in the early republic
was essentially conceived of in corporate terms and the institu-
tions created at the founding of our nation were not intended to
threaten this arrangement. They were meant to secure the local
communities from the threat of central tyranny, but were not concerned with the tyranny that often existed within each subcultural
unit. Roche argues that this pattern has broken down and attri-
butes its demise to urbanization, industrialization and the rise
of elites concerned with civil liberties that have "infiltrated"
the ever more powerful national government. The effect has been
to produce a new pattern; a society marked by impersonality and
the bureaucratization of interpersonal and intergroup conflict.[32]

All of this can be put another way. The older pattern is one
in which Americans are grouped into geographic subcultures of
shared attitudes and intolerant dispositions possessing direct
majority control of the local political and legal apparatus, thus
insuring institutional support or acquiescence for their point of
view. This situation is possible only when the degree of economic
and political interdependence required on a national basis is minimal. Such was the case in an America with a rural economy shielded
from serious problems of national defense by two large oceans and
weak neighbors.

The economic requirements of modern industrial America stress
interdependence. People with skills are required; they must move
to places where their skills are needed; large numbers of people

must live, work and educate themselves in densely populated urban areas. Modern transportation and communication produce constant subcultural interpenetration. It thus becomes increasingly difficult for a subculture to encompass its members in a limited geographic area. Persons affiliated with one or another of these subcultures are increasingly required to spend a large amount of their time together with members of other subcultures in activities to which the subcultural affiliation is essentially irrelevant.

But the subcultures do not all disappear; many persist and many new ones form. And although what Roche terms the "bureaucratization of civil liberties" tends to reinforce the perspective of a series of individuals claiming arbitrary or discriminatory treatment, on the whole the major attacks upon and victories for civil liberties remain, at root, group conflicts. The frequent inability to obtain satisfactory results from state and local governments which retain the relevant police powers and often use them to reinforce the older pattern, has led many groups to seek national intervention to secure their equal rights. Operating, in a sense, as the agent of the newer pattern, the Supreme Court has increasingly used the Fourteenth Amendment as a vehicle to extend basic liberties to these political, racial and cultural minorities.

The Proper Function of Fourteenth Amendment Enforcement

The traditional perspective on the Fourteenth Amendment which views it as a vehicle for the strengthening of individual rights and liberties remains unquestioned, but the Amendment should also be viewed as a reflection of and instrument for the development of a new national pattern of intergroup relationships in America. It is therefore appropriate for the national government to protect, from private as well as state action, citizens who suffer attacks on or deprivations of all basic rights because of their group "affiliation." It may be plausibly argued that an attack on a person because of his "affiliation" -- racial, political, or cultural -- has a dimension to it that is lacking in an ordinary criminal act. The latter, of course, involves a deprivation of rights to the individual victim and an assault on his dignity as a free citizen of a democracy. In that sense all acts of criminal violence are technically political. But acts directed against people because of their perceived group membership are not just technically political. The pattern of group interest is a prime basis of our politics; our civil liberties amendments and laws are institutional arrangements that both shape and are determined by this pattern of group interest and conflict. Thus such an attack is political in a much broader sense than the ordinary criminal act. In addition to constituting an assault on fundamental public order, it attacks the ongoing process of institutionalizing a pattern of pluralism that provides for the free formation, survival and/or competition of varied political, racial and cultural groups in our nation.

Because this is a national process and one in which the federal government has historically played a dominant role, it is appropriate that those crimes which also represent an attack on the process be subject to its concurrent jurisdiction. From this perspective, the constitutional congressional power to enforce directly the Fourteenth Amendment should be seen as covering assaults on the rights of individuals from any quarter that are due to the victim's group affiliation. Indeed if this is done, then the vague assertions of Reconstruction legislators and judges about a distinction between ordinary crimes and crimes that deprive one of one's civil rights, a distinction which seems so hard to make when rights are looked upon solely as the accoutrements of individual dignity, would finally become more meaningful.

Senator Edmunds, defending his amendment to the 1871 Enforcement Act,[33] made such a distinction. While one cannot single out one favorable expression of congressional opinion from the many and contradictory speeches of the Reconstruction period as uniquely valid, this quotation, as well as some notable remarks of Supreme Court Justice Joseph P. Bradley[34] and Congressman (later President) James A. Garfield,[35] suggests that a "group affiliation" approach seems to have commended itself to some important persons contemporary with passage and early enforcement of the Fourteenth Amendment. Edmunds said,

> We do not undertake in this bill to interfere with
> what might be called a private conspiracy growing
> out of a neighborhood feud of one man or a set of
> men against another...; but, if...it should appear
> that the conspiracy was formed against this man
> because he was a Democrat, if you please, or be-
> cause he was a Catholic, or because he was a
> Methodist, or because he was a Vermonter...then
> this section could reach it.[36]

"Group affiliation" or "class" as a distinguishing concept, as a method of drawing a line around national power to enforce Fourteenth Amendment protection of basic rights, resolves the dilemma in such enforcement. Federal power to protect directly Fourteenth Amendment rights against private interference would extend to situations involving the deprivation of any rights which the court has come to

VERNON REGIONAL
JUNIOR COLLEGE LIBRARY

recognize as part of the life, liberty and property that states may not deny without due process of law. But the enforcement power would be confined to deprivations that are due to the "group affiliation" of the victim. Enforcement statutes would presumably be drawn to cover attacks directed at people because of race, religion, national origin or political affiliation but they could also cover other kinds of "classifications" as well. They would not reach most ordinary crimes because such crimes are not normally committed against a victim because of his "group" affiliation.[37] Whether the federal government would want to extend its power to the outer limits of the "group affiliation" concept would depend upon the national political situation.[38] The point is, there would be valid limits although their exact location might be a matter of debate and the federal government's potential role would be very extensive.

For the Court to decide that Congress has the Fourteenth Amendment enforcement authority to reach private action concurrently with (or even superseding) the states, but only when improper considerations of group affiliation are involved in the deprivation of rights, would not be an arbitrary limitation. It would be one well grounded in the historical functioning of the Amendment in the developing American society. And it offers a way to empower the Congress to protect the civil rights and liberties of all groups while maintaining a reasonable and appropriate balance within the federal system.

SECTION III - References

1. Archibald Cox, "Foreword: Constitutional Adjudication and the Promotion of Human Rights," Harvard Law Review, Vol. 80; (1966), p. 61.

2. 383 U.S. 301 (1966).

3. 384 U.S. 641 (1966).

4. 383 U.S. 745 (1966).

5. In South Carolina v. Katzenbach the Court sustained the Voting Rights Act of 1965 by reading a "necessary and proper clause" into the enforcement provisions of the Fifteenth Amendment; the language of the Fifteenth Amendment enforcement provisions is essentially the same as that of the Fourteenth Amendment. In Katzenbach v. Morgan, the Court held that Congress could set aside state voting requirements of English literacy if, in Congress' judgment, such action was necessary to insure equal protection of basic rights of the Spanish speaking; this was appropriate action under the Fourteenth Amendment's enforcement provisions. In U.S. v. Guest six justices went out of their way to indicate that in their view, the scope of Congress' Fourteenth Amendment enforcement power was not limited by the then traditional view that Congress could reach only state action, not private action. From all this Cox saw no logical limitation upon the power of Congress to take whatever action is deemed necessary and proper to secure any or all Fourteenth Amendment rights. (Amendment XIV, Section 5 simply states: "The Congress shall have the power to enforce, by appropriate legislation, the provisions of this article.")

6. Cox, op. cit., p. 99-108, 118-119.

7. 109 U.S. 3 (1183).

8. Cox, op. cit., p. 155; see also, "Can Congress Abolish the State?" California Law Review, Vol. 20 (1967), p. 293. The problem arises if Congress has the power to secure against the world all individual rights to life, liberty and property. Such rights are really the reciprocal of the state police power and their full enforcement by the national government would leave little for the states to do.

9. Cox, op. cit., p. 118-120, The full exercise by Congress of such sweeping powers would have to be preceded by an extraordinary shift in the nation's politics. Cox points out that for political reasons, Congress has not seen fit to exercise the full range of its authority under the post-1936 interpretation of the Interstate Commerce Clause.

10. Jones v. Mayer, 392 U.S. 409 (1968). The Court interpreted the provisions of the successor to the Civil Rights Act of 1866, which confers upon the Blacks the same rights to make contracts as other citizens, to mean that Whites may not refuse to contract to sell their private residences to Black would-be purchasers. This statute is based upon the Thirteenth Amendment; it reaches private acts of racial discrimination on the theory that they are vestiges of slavery which Congress may eradicate under the authority granted by the Thirteenth Amendment's enforcement clause.

11. It is true that the Thirteenth Amendment can evidently support statutes that protect Whites against race discrimination too. The Court upheld the use of a statute based upon the Thirteenth Amendment for such a purpose in MacDonald v. Santa Fe Transportation Co., 427 U.S. 273 (1976).

12. A priority which is, of course, fully justified.

13. (New York: Macmillan, 1963).

14. Ibid, p. 36.

15. Ibid, p. 91 (Emphasis Added).

16. J. Legler, Toleration and the Reformation, (2 Vols. New York: Association Press, 1960).

17. John P. Roche, Courts and Rights, (New York: Random House, 1966) pp. 56-61.

18. William Riker, Democracy in the U.S., (New York: Macmillan, 1963) p. 92.

19. Ibid.

20. Riker, op. cit., p. 91.

21. For example, in Thomas Emerson, Toward a General Theory of the First Amendment, (New York: Vintage Books, 1966), the first chapter entitled "The Function of Freedom of Expression

in a Democratic Society" begins: "The right of the individual
to freedom of expression...," p. 3; Henry Abraham, Freedom
and the Court: Civil Rights and Liberties in the U.S. (New
York; Oxford University Press, 1967) begins in the preface
with: "This is essentially a study of the lines that must
be drawn by a democratic society as it attempts to reconcile
individual freedom with the rights of the community." And
the civil liberties chapter of Charles Black, Perspectives
on Constitutional Law (Englewood Cliffs: Prentice-Hall, 1963)
is entitled: "Individual Rights Against Government," p. 76.

22. "The Fourteenth Amendment ... marked an extension of federal
authority, a more toward uniformity throughout the nation in
matters of civil liberty, to be attained by authority of the
federal government." Alexander Bickel, The Least Dangerous
Branch, (Indianapolis: Bobbs-Merrill, 1962), p. 101.

23. See for example, Anthony Lewis, Gideon's Trumpet, (New York:
Vintage Books, 1964).

24. F. N. Thorpe, Federal and State Constitutions, Colonial Charters and Other Organic Laws of the States, Territories and
Colonies Now or Heretofor Forming the United States of America
(Washington: Government Printing Office, 1909) (Vols. I
through VII); B. P. Poore, Federal and State Constitutions,
Colonial Charters and Other Organic Laws of the U.S. (Washington: Government Printing Office, 1877; Index Digest of
State Constitutions, (Albany, NY: New York State Constitutional Commission, 1915).

25. For example: Wisconsin v. Yoder, 406 U.S. 205 (1972) — the
"Amish"; Sherbert v. Verner, 374 U.S. 398 (1963) — Seventh
Day Adventists; West Virginia v. Barnette, 319 U.S. 624
(1943) — Jehovah's Witnesses; Brandenburg v. Ohio, 395 U.S.
444 (1969) — Ku Klux Klan; Edwards v. South Carolina, 372
U.S. 229 (1963) — Black Civil Rights Demonstrators; Tinker
v. Des Moines, 393 U.S. 503 (1969) — Anti-Viet Nam War
Protestors.

26. Gideon v. Wainwright, 372 U.S. 335 (1963); Griffen v. Illinois,
351 U.S. 12 (1956); Goldberg v. Kelly, 397 U.S. 254 (1970);
Miranda v. Arizona, 384 U.S. 436 (1966); Sinadach v. Family
Finance Corp. 395 U.S. 337 (1969).

27. See for example, Clement Vose, "Litigation as a Form of
Pressure Group Activity," Annals of the American Academy
of Political and Social Science, Vol. 319 (1958), p. 20; Vose,

"The National Consumers League and the Brandeis Brief," Midwest Journal of Political Science, Vol. I (1957), p. 276; Vose, Caucasions Only: The Supreme Court, the N.A.A.C.P., and the Restrictive Covenant Cases (Berkeley: University of California Press, 1959); Hackman, "Lobbying the Supreme Court An Appraisal of Political Science Folklore," Fordham Law Review, Vol. 35 (1966) p. 15.

28. John Roche, The Quest for the Dream (New York: MacMillan, 1963); John Roche, "American Liberty: An Examination of the Tradition of Freedom," "We've Never had more Freedom," Shadow and Substance (New York: Collier Books (1964) pp. 3,39.

29. Roche, Shadow and Substance, pp. 8-9.

30. Roche, The Quest for the Dream, p. 8.

31. Andrew Hacker, The End of the American Era (New York: Atherton, 1970) p. 209.

32. Roche, Shadow and Substance, pp. 28-30, 32.

33. The Ku Klux Klan Act, of April 20, 1871, 17 Stat. 13, See also footnote 37 below.

34. See: John Roche, "Civil Liberty in the Age of Enterprise," University of Chicago Law Review, Vol. 31 (1963) pp. 103, 108-110; U.S. v. Cruikshank, 1 Woods 308, 25 Fed. Cas. 707 (No. 14, 897) (1874).

35. Congressional Globe, 42nd Congress, 1st Session (1871), Appendix, pp. 150-153.

36. Congressional Globe, 42nd Congress, 1st Session (1871), pp. 566-567.

37. Since the primary purpose of this article is to establish the validity of the pluralist perspective and not distract the reader with the technical problems of basing enforcement statutes on group affiliation, I have not discussed them. But any who are sceptical or who think it impractical should know that the concept is actually used, as a result of Supreme Court interpretation of Congressional intent, in 42 U.S.C. 1985 (3). In Griffen v. Breckenridge 403 U.S. 88 (1971) the Supreme Court, reviving the long neglected

conspiracy section which originated in the 1871 Civil Rights Act, held that it could be used to reach certain purely private conspiracies to deprive persons of their equal enjoyment of legal rights. According to the Court, to state a valid claim under the statue a plaintiff must allege "some racial, or perhaps otherwise class-based invidiously discriminatory animus." 403 U.S. 88, 102.

38. Some may react that since women's rights advocates would demand that all rapes be covered, and since many muggings have racial overtones, the group affiliation concept will not keep the federal government out of ordinary crimes. My response is that if Congress, adopting a pluralist perspective, concludes that such crimes threaten the developing American pattern of inter-group relations and wishes to "federalize" them, then so be it; they are not then, ordinary crimes.

APPENDIX

A. EXTRACTS FROM MAJOR CONGRESSIONAL LEGISLATION
ARGUABLY DESIGNED TO PREVENT PRIVATE INTERFERENCE
WITH CIVIL AND VOTING RIGHTS UNDER THE AUTHORITY
OF THE THIRTEENTH, FOURTEENTH AND
FIFTEENTH AMENDMENTS

I. THE CIVIL RIGHTS ACT OF 1866.

        Act of April 9, 1966. 14 Stat. 27.

        --An Act to protect all Persons in the
        United States in their Civil Rights, and
        furnish the Means of their Vindication.

    [SECTION 1.] Be it enacted by the Senate and
House of Representatives of the United States of
America in Congress assembled, That all persons
born in the United States and not subject to any
foreign power, excluding Indians not taxed, are
hereby declared to be citizens of the United States;
and such citizens, of every race and color, without regard to any previous condition of slavery or
involuntary servitude, except as a punishment for
crime whereof the party shall have been duly convicted, shall have the same right, in every State
and Territory in the United States, to make and
enforce contracts, to sue, be parties, and give
evidence, to inherit, purchase, lease, sell, hold,
and convey real and personal property, and to full
and equal benefit of all laws and proceedings for
the security of person and property, as is enjoyed
by white citizens, and shall be subject to like
punishment, pains, and penalties, and to none other,
any law, statute, ordinance, regulation, or custom,
to the contrary notwithstanding.

    SECTION 2. And be it further enacted, That any
person who, under color of any law, statute, ordinance, regulation, or custom, shall subject, or

cause to be subjected, any inhabitant of any State
or Territory to the deprivation of any right secured or protected by this act, or to different
punishment, pains, or penalties on account of such
person having at any time been held in a condition
of slavery of involuntary servitude, except as a
punishment for crime whereof the party shall have
been duly convicted, or by reason of his color or
race, than is prescribed for the punishment of
white persons, shall be deemed guilty of a misdemeanor, and, on conviction, shall be punished by
fine not exceeding one thousand dollars, or imprisonment not exceeding one year, or both, in the discretion of the court.

II. THE ENFORCEMENT ACT OF 1870.

Act of May 31, 1870. 16 Stat. 140.

--An Act to enforce the Right of Citizens
of the United States to vote in the several States of this Union, and for other
purposes.

. . . .

SECTION 5. And be it further enacted, That if
any person shall prevent, hinder, control, or intimidate, or shall attempt to prevent, hinder, control,
or intimidate, any person from exercising or in exercising the right of suffrage, to whom the right
of suffrage is secured or guaranteed by the fifteenth amendment to the Constitution of the United
States, by means of bribery, threats, or threats
of depriving such person of employment or occupa-
tion, or of ejecting such person from rented house,
lands, or other property, or by threats of violence
to himself or family, such person so offending shall
be deemed guilty of a misdemeanor, and shall, on
conviction thereof, be fined not less than five
hundred dollars, or be imprisoned not less than one
month and not more than one year, or both, at the
discretion of the court.

SECTION 6. And be it further enacted, That if
two or more persons shall band or conspire together or go in disguise upon the public highway, or
upon the premises of another, with intent to violate any provision of this act, or to injure, op-

- 82 -

press, threaten, or intimidate any citizen with intent to prevent or hinder his free exercise and enjoyment of any right of privilege granted or secured to him by the Constitution or law of the United States, or because of his having exercised the same, such persons shall be held guilty of felony, and, on conviction thereof, shall be fined or imprisoned, or both, at the discretion of the court, --the fine not to exceed five thousand dollars, and the imprisonment not to exceed ten years, --and shall, moreover, be thereafter ineligible to, and disabled from holding, any office or place of honor, profit, or trust created by the Constitution or laws of the United States.

SECTION 7. And be it further enacted, That if in the act of violating any provision in either of the two preceding sections, any other felony, crime, or misdemeanor shall be committed, the offender, on conviction of such violation of said sections, shall be punished for the same with such punishments as are attached to the said felonies, crimes, and misdemeanors by the laws of the State in which the offense may be committed.

III.   THE KU KLUX KLAN ACT.

Act of April 20, 1871.   17 Stat. 13.

--An Act to enforce the Provisions of the Fourteenth Amendment to the Constitution of the United States, and for other Purposes.

. . . .

SECTION 2. That if two or more persons within any State or Territory of the United States shall conspire together to overthrow or to put down, or to destroy by force the government of the United States, or to levy war against the United States, or to oppose by force the authority of the government of the United States, or by force, intimidation, or threat to prevent, hinder, or delay the execution of any law of the United States, or by force to seize, take, or possess any property of the United States contrary to the authority there-

of, or by force, intimidation, or threat to prevent any person from accepting or holding any office or trust or place of confidence under the
United States, or from discharging the duties thereof, or by force, intimidation, or threat to induce
any officer of the United States to leave any State,
district, or place where his duties as such officer
might lawfully be performed, or to injure him in
his person or property on account of his lawful
discharge of the duties of his office, or to injure
his person while engaged in the lawful discharge
of the duties of his office, or to injure his property so as to molest, interrupt, hinder, or impede
him in the discharge of his official duty, or by
force, intimidation, or threat to deter any party
or witness in any court of the United States from
attending such court, or from testifying in any
matter pending in such court fully, freely, and
truthfully, or to injure any such party or witness
in his person or property on account of his having
so attended or testified, or by force, intimidation, or threat to influence the verdict, presentment, or indictment, of any juror or grand juror
in any court of the United States, or to injure
such juror in his person or property on account
of any verdict, presentment, or indictment lawfully assented to by him, or on account of his
being or having been such juror, or shall conspire
together, or go in disguise upon the public highway or upon the premises of another for the purpose,
either directly or indirectly, of depriving any
person or any class of persons of the equal protection of the laws, or of equal privileges or
immunities under the laws, or for the purpose of
preventing or hindering the constituted authorities of any State from giving or securing to all
persons within such State the equal protection of
the laws, or shall conspire together for the purpose of in any manner impeding, hindering, obstruc-
ting, or defeating the due course of justice in
any State or Territory, with intent to deny to any
citizen of the United States the due and equal
protection of the laws, or to injure in his person
or property for lawfully enforcing the right of any
person or class of persons to the equal protection
of the laws, or by force, intimidation, or threat
to prevent any citizen of the United States enti-

tled to vote from giving his support or advocacy
in a lawful manner towards or in favor of the election of any lawfully qualified persons as an elector of President or Vice-President of the United
States, or as a member of the Congress of the United States, or to injure any such citizen in his
person or property on account of such support or
advocacy, each and every person so offending shall
be deemed guilty of a high crime, upon conviction
thereof in any district or circuit court of the
United States or district or supreme court of any
Territory of the United States having jurisdiction
of similar offences, shall be punished by a fine
not less than five hundred nor more than five
thousand dollars, or by imprisonment, with or without hard labor, as the court may determine, for a
period of not less than six months nor more than
six years, as the court may determine, or by both
such fine and imprisonment as the court shall determine. And if any one or more persons engaged
in any such conspiracy shall do, or cause to be
done, any act in furtherance of the object of such
conspiracy, whereby any person shall be injured in
his person or deprived of having and exercising
any right or privilege of a citizen of the United
States, the person so injured or deprived of such
rights and privileges may have and maintain an action for the recovery of damages occasioned by such
injury or deprivation of rights and privileges a-
gainst any one or more of the persons engaged in
such conspiracy, such action to be prosecuted in the
proper district or circuit court, of the United
States, with and subject to the same rights of ap-
peal, review upon error, and other remedies provided in like cases in such courts under the provisions of the act of April ninth, eighteen hundred
and sixty-six, entitled, "An act to protect all persons in the United States in their civil rights,
and to furnish the means of their vindication."

SECTION 3. That in all cases where insurrection, domestic violence, unlawful combinations, or
conspiracies in any State shall so obstruct or hinder the execution of the laws thereof, and of the
United States, as to deprive any portion or class
of the people of such State of any of the rights,

privileges, or immunities, or protection, named in
the Constitution and secured by this act, and the
constituted authorities of such State shall either
be unable to protect, or shall, from any cause,
fail in or refuse protection of the people in such
rights, such facts shall be deemed a denial by such
State of the equal protection of the laws to which
they are entitled under the Constitution of the
United States; and in all cases, or whenever any
such insurrection, violence, unlawful combination,
or conspiracy shall oppose or obstruct the laws of
the United States or the due execution thereof, or
impede or obstruct the due course of justice under
the same, it shall be lawful for the President, and
it shall be his duty to take such measures, by the
employment of the militia or the land and naval forces
of the United States, or of either, or by other means,
as he may deem necessary for the suppression of
such insurrection, domestic violence, or combinations; and any person who shall be arrested under
the provisions of this and the preceding section
shall be delivered to the marshal of the proper
district, to be dealt with according to law.

SECTION 4. That whenever in any State or part
of a State the unlawful combinations named in the
preceding section of this act shall be organized
and armed, and so numerous and powerful as to be
able, by violence, to either overthrow or set at
defiance the constituted authorities of such State,
and of the United States within such State, or
when the constituted authorities are in complici-
ty with, or shall connive at the unlawful purposes of, such powerful and armed combinations;
and whenever, by reason of either or all of the
causes aforesaid, the conviction of such offenders
and the preservation of the public safety shall
become in such district impracticable, in every
such case such combinations shall be deemed a
rebellion against the government of the United
States, and during the continuance of such rebellion, and within the limits of the district which
shall be so under the sway thereof, such limits to
be prescribed by proclamation, it shall be lawful
for the President of the United States, when in
his judgment the public safety shall require it,
to suspend the privileges of the writ of habeas
corpus, to the end that such rebellion may be
overthrown: Provided, That all the provisions of

the second section of an act entitled "An act
relating to habeas corpus, and regulating judicial
proceedings in certain cases," approved March third,
eighteen hundred and sixty-three, which relate to
the discharge of prisoners other than prisoners
of war, and to the penalty for refusing to obey
the order of the court, shall be in full force so
far as the same are applicable to the provisions
of this section: Provided further, That the President shall first have made proclamation, as now
provided by law, commanding such insurgents to dis-
perse: And provided also, That the provisions of
this section shall not be in force after the end
of the next regular session of Congress.

IV.   THE CIVIL RIGHTS ACT OF 1875.

         Act of March 1, 1875. 18 Stat. 335.

         --An Act to protect all citizens in their
         civil and legal rights.

     Whereas, it is essential to just government we
recognize the equality of all men before the law,
and hold that it is the duty of government in its
dealings with the people to mete out equal and
exact justice to all, of whatever nativity, race,
color, or persuasion, religious or political; and
it being the appropriate object of legislation to
enact great fundamental principles into law:
Therefore,

     Be it enacted by the Senate and House of Repre-
sentatives of the United States of America in Congress assembled. That all persons within the jurisdiction of the United States shall be entitled to
the full and equal enjoyment of the accommodations,
advantages, facilities, and privileges of inns,
public conveyances, on land or water, theatres, and
other places of public amusement; subject only to
the conditions and limitations established by law,
and applicable alike to citizens of every race and
color, regardless of any previous condition of servitude.

SECTION 2. That any person who shall violate
the foregoing section by denying to any citizen,
except for reasons by law applicable to citizens
of every race and color, and regardless of any previous condition of servitude, the full enjoyment of
any of the accommodations, advantages, or privileges
in said section enumerated, or by aiding or inciting such denial, shall, for every such offense, for-
feit and pay the sum of five hundred dollars to the
person aggrieved thereby, to be recovered in an
action of debt, with full costs; and shall also,
for every such offense, be deemed guilty of a misdemeanor, and, upon conviction thereof, shall be
fined not less than five hundred nor more than one
thousand dollars, or shall be imprisoned not less
than thirty days nor more than one year: Provided,
That all persons may elect to sue for the penalty
aforesaid or to proceed under their rights at common law and by State statutes; and having so elected to proceed in the one mode or the other, their
right to proceed in the other jurisdiction shall
be barred. But this proviso shall not apply to
criminal proceedings, either under this act or the
criminal law of any State: And provided further,
That a judgment for the penalty in favor of the
party aggrieved, or a judgment upon an indictment,
shall be a bar to either prosecution respectively.

V. THE CIVIL RIGHTS ACT OF 1968.

        Act of April 11, 1968. 82 Stat. 73.

        --To prescribe penalties for certain acts
        of violence or intimidation, and for
        other purposes.

    Be it enacted by the Senate and House of Rep-
resentatives of the United States of America assembled,

_ 88 _

TITLE I --INTERFERENCE WITH FEDERALLY
          PROTECTED ACTIVITIES

SECTION 101.

(a) That chapter 13, civil rights, title 18,
    United States Code, is amended by inser-
    ting immediately at the end thereof the
    following new section, to read as follows:

    "SECTION 245. Federally protected activi-
    ties

            . . . .

    "(b) Whoever, whether or not acting under
         color of law, by force or threat of
         force willfully injures, intimidates
         or interferes with, or attempts to
         injure, intimidate or interfere with--

         "(1) any person because he is or has
              been, or in order to intimidate
              such person or any other person
              or any class of persons from --

              "(A) voting or qualifying to
                   vote, qualifying or cam-
                   paigning as a candidate
                   for elective office, or
                   qualifying or acting as
                   a poll watcher, or any
                   legally authorized elec-
                   tion official, in any pri-
                   mary, special, or general
                   election;

"(B) participating in or enjoying any benefit, service,
privilege, program, facility, or activity provided
or administered by the
United States;

"(C) applying for or enjoying
employment, or any perqui-
site thereof, by any agency
of the United States;

"(D) serving, or attending upon
any court in connection
with possible service, as
a grand or petit juror in
any court of the United
States;

"(E) participating in or enjoying the benefits of any program or activity receiving
Federal financial assis-
tance; or

"(2) any person because of his race,
color, religion, or national
origin and because he is or has
been --

"(A) enrolling in or attending
any public school or public
college.

"(B) participating in or enjoying any benefit, service,
privilege, program, facility
or activity provided or
administered by any State
or subdivision thereof;

"(C) applying for or enjoying
employment, or any per-
quisite thereof, by any
private employer or any
agency of any State or subdivision thereof, or joining
or using the services or
advantages of any labor organization, hiring hall, or
employment agency;

"(D) serving, or attending upon
any court of any State in
connection with possible
service, as a grand or petit
juror;

"(E) traveling in or using any
facility of interstate commerce, or using any vehicle,
terminal, or facility of any
common carrier by motor,
rail, water, or air;

"(F) enjoying the goods, services,
facilities, privileges, advantages, or accommodations
of any inn, hotel, motel, or
other establishment which
provides lodging to transient
guests, or of any restaurant,
cafeteria, lunchroom, lunch
counter, soda fountain, or
other facility which serves
the public and which is prin-
cipally engaged in selling
food or beverages for consump-
tion on the premises, or
of any gasoline station, or
of any motion picture house,

theater, concert hall,
sports arena, stadium, or
any other place of exhibi-
tion or entertainment which
serves the public, or of
any other establishment
which serves the public and
(i) which is located within
the premises of any of the
aforesaid establishments or
within the premises of which
is physically located any
of the aforesaid establishments, and (ii) which holds
itself out as serving pat-
rons of such establishments;
or

"(3) during or incident to a riot or
civil disorder, any person engaged in a business in commerce
or affecting commerce, including,
but not limited to, any person
engaged in a business which sells
or offers for sale to interstate
travelers a substantial portion
of the articles, commodities, or
services which it sells or where
a substantial portion of the articles or commodities which it sells
or offers for sale have moved in
commerce; or

"(4) any person because he is or has
been, or in order to intimidate
such person or any other person
or any class of persons from --

"(A) participating, without discrimination on account of
race, color, religion, or

national origin, in any of
the benefits or activities
described in subparagraphs
(1)(A) through (1)(E) or
subparagraphs (2)(A) through
(2)(F); or

"(B) affording another person or
class of persons opportunity
or protection to so participate; or

"(5) any citizen because he is or has
been, or in order to intimidate
such citizen or any other citizen from unlawfully aiding or
encouraging other persons to participate, without discrimination
on account of race, color, religion or national origin, in any
of the benefits or activities
described in subparagraphs (1)(A)
through (1)(E) or subparagraphs
(2)(A) through (2)(F), or participating lawfully in speech or
peaceful assembly opposing any
denial of the opportunity to so
participate --

shall be fined not more than $1,000,
or imprisoned not more than one year,
or both; and if bodily injury results
shall be fined not more than $10,000,
or imprisoned not more than ten years,
or both; and if death results shall
be subject to imprisonment for any
term of years or for life. As used
in this section, the term 'participating lawfully in speech or peaceful assembly' shall not mean the
aiding, abetting, or inciting of
other persons to riot or to commit
any act of physical violence upon any
individual or against any real or

personal property in furtherance of a riot. Nothing in sub-
paragraph (2)(F) or (4)(A) of this
subsection shall apply to the proprietor of any establishment which
provides lodging to transient guests,
or to any employee acting on behalf
of such proprietor, with respect to
enjoyment of the goods, services,
facilities, privileges, advantages,
or accommodations of such establishments is located within a building
which contains not more than five
rooms for rent or hire and which is
actually occupied by the proprietor.

"(c) Nothing in this section shall be
construed so as to deter any law
enforcement officer from lawfully
carrying out the duties of his office;
and no law enforcement officer shall
be considered to be in violation of
this section for lawfully carrying
out the duties of his office or lawfully enforcing ordinances and laws
of the United States, the District
of Columbia, any of the several States,
or any political subdivision of a
State. For purposes of the preceding
sentence, the term 'law enforcement
officer' means any officer of the
United States, the District of Columbia, a State, or political subdivision of a State, who is empowered
by law to conduct investigations of,
or make arrests because of, offenses
against the United States, the District of Columbia, a State, or a political subdivision of a State."

(b) Nothing contained in this section shall
apply to or affect activities under
Title VIII of this Act.

(c) The provisions of this section shall not
    apply to acts or omissions on the part
    of law enforcement officers, members of
    the National Guard, as defined in sec-
    tion 101 (9) of Title 10, United States
    Code, members of the organized militia of
    any State, or the District of Columbia,
    not covered by such section 101 (9), or
    members of the Armed Forces of the United
    States, who are engaged in suppressing a
    riot or civil disturbance or restoring
    law and order during a riot or civil
    disturbance.

                . . . .

SECTION 103.

(a) Section 241 of Title 18, United States
    Code, is amended by striking out the
    final paragraph thereof and substituting
    the following:

        "They shall be fined not more
        than $10,000, or imprisoned
        not more than ten years, or both;
        and if death results, they shall
        be subject to imprisonment for
        any term of years or for life."

(b) Section 242 of Title 18, United States
    Code, is amended by striking out the period
    at the end thereof and adding the follow-
    ing: "; and if death results shall be
    subject to imprisonment for any term of
    years or for life."

B. BIBLIOGRAPHY

I. Official Reports, Documents and Government Publications

1. Civil Rights, Hearings of the Subcommittee on Constitutional Rights of the Committee on the Judiciary, 89th Congress, 2nd Session, 1966.

2. Congressional Globe, 39th Congress, 1st Session, 1866; 40th Congress, 3rd Session, 1870; 41st Congress, 2nd Session, 1871; 42nd Congress, 1st Session, Appendix, 1872.

3. The Constitution of the United States.

4. Kendrick, Benjamin (ed), The Journal of the Joint Committee of Fifteen on Reconstruction, 39th Congress, 1865-1867, Columbia University Studies in History, Economics, and Public Law. Vol. LXII, New York: Columbia University Press, 1914.

5. Ninth Annual Report, Advisory Commission on Intergovernmental Relations, Washington, D.C.: U.S. Government Printing Office 1968.

6. Report of the Attorney-General, 1870-1875.

7. Report of the Joint Committee on Reconstruction, 39th Congress, 1st Session, 1865.

8. Unites States Commission on Civil Rights, Freedom to the Free, Washington, D.C.: U.S. Government Printing Office, 1963.

9. United States Commission on Civil Rights, Justice, Washington, D.C.: U.S. Government Printing Office, 1961.

10. United States Commission on Civil Rights, Law Enforcement- A Report on Equal Protection in the South, Washington, D.C.: U.S. Government Printing Office, 1965.

11. United States Reports, Volumes 3-428.

12. United States Statutes at Large.

II. Books and Articles

1. "A Note on Statutory Interpretation," Harvard Law Review,
   Vol. 43, 1930.

2. Becker, Theodore (ed.), The Impact of Supreme Court Decisions, New York: Oxford University Press, 1969.

3. Bennett, Lerone Jr., Confrontation: Black and White,
   Baltimore: Penguin Books, 1968.

4. Bickel, Alexander, The Least Dangerous Branch, Indianapolis:
   Bobbs-Merrill, 1962.

5. _____, "The Original Understanding and the Segregation Decision," Harvard Law Review, Vol. 65, 1955.

6. _____, The Supreme Court and the Idea of Progress, New York:
   Harper and Row, 1970.

7. Black, Charles, Perspectives on Constitutional Law, Englewood
   Cliffs: Prentice-Hall, 1963.

8. Blaustein and Zangrando, Civil Rights and the American Negro,
   New York: Washington Square Press, 1968.

9. Branch, Taylor, "Black Fear: Law and Justice in Rural Georgia,"
   Washington Monthly, January, 1970.

10. "Can Congress Abolish the States"? California Law Review,
    Vol. 20, 1967.

11. Carr, Bernstein and Murphy, Essentials of American Democracy,
    New York: Rolt, Rinehart and Winston, 1968.

12. Carr, Robert, Federal Protection of Civil Rights, Ithaca:
    Cornell University Press, 1947.

13. Cater, Douglas, Power in Washington, New York: Vintage, 1964.

14. Connolly, William E. (ed.), The Bias of Pluralism, New York,
    Atherton Press, 1969.

15. Corwin, Edward, The "Higher Law" Background of American Con-
    stitutional Law, Ithaca: Cornell University Press, 1955.

16. Cox, Archibald, "Foreword: Constitutional Adjudication and the Promotion of Human Rights," Harvard Law Review, Vol. 80, 1966.

17. _____, The Warren Court, Cambridge: Harvard University Press, 1968.

18. Cummings and McFarland, Federal Justice, New York: McMillan Co., 1937.

19. Dahl, Robert, Pluralist Democracy in the United States, Chicago: Rand McNally, 1967.

20. _____, Who Governs? New Haven: Yale University Press, 1961.

21. DeTocqueville, Alexis, Democracy in the United States, 2 Vols. New York: Vintage Books, 1945.

22. "Developments in the Law -- Equal Protection," Harvard Law Review, Vol 82, 1969.

23. Dorsen, Normal, Discrimination and Civil Rights, Boston: Little, Brown and Co., 1969.

24. Emerson, Thomas, Toward A General Theory of the First Amendment, New York: Random House Vintage, 1966.

25. Fairman, Charles, "Does the Fourteenth Amendment Incorporate the Bill of Rights: The Original Understanding," Stanford Law Review, Vol. 5, 1949.

26. Farnsworth, Allan, An Introduction to the Legal System of the United States, New York: Oceana Publications, 1951.

27. Flack, Horace, The Adoption of the Fourteenth Amendment, Baltimore; The Johns Hopkins Press, 1908.

28. Frank and Munro, "The Original Understanding of 'Equal Protection of the Laws,'" Columbia Law Review, Vol. 50, 1950.

29. Franklin, John Hope, Reconstruction After the Civil War, Chicago: University of Chicago Press, 1961.

30. Frantz, L. B., "Congressional Power to Enforce the Fourteenth Amendment Against Private Acts," Yale Law Journal, Vol. 73, 1964.

31. Freidrich, Carl, Trends of Federalism in Theory and Practice, New York: Praeger, 1968.

32. Freund et al., Constitutional Law, Boston: Little, Brown and Co., 1961.

33. Fuller, Lon. Anatomy of the Law, New York: Praeger, 1968.

34. Graham, Howard J., "Our 'Declaratory' Fourteenth Amendment," Stanford Law Review, Vol. 7, 1954.

35. _____, "The Conspiracy Theory of the Fourteenth Amendment," Yale Law Journal, Vol. 47, 48, 1968.

36. Harris, Robert, The Search for Equality, BatonRouge: Louisiana State University Press, 1960.

37. Hart and Sacks, The Legal Process, Cambridge: Harvard Law School, Tentative Edition, 1958.

38. Howe, Cox and Wiggens, Civil Rights, The Constitution and the Press, Cambridge: Harvard University Press, 1967.

39. Huston, Luther A., et al., Roles of the Attorney-General of The United States, Washington, D.C. American Enterprises Institute, 1968.

40. Jacob, H. Politics and the Federal Courts, Boston: Little, Brown, and Co., 1967.

41. James, Joseph, The Framing of the Fourteenth Amendment, Urbana: University of Illinois Press, 1956.

42. Kariel, Harry, The Decline of American Pluralism, Stanford, Stanford University Press, 1967.

43. Konvitz, Milton, Expanding Liberties, New York: Viking Press, 1966.

44. Kutler, B., Judicial Power and Reconstruction Politics, Chicago: University of Chicago Press, 1968.

45. Lewis, Anthony, Gideon's Trumpet, New York: Random House Vintage, 1964.

46. Litt, Edgar, Beyond Pluralism: Ethnic Politics in America, New York: Scott, Foresman, 1970.

47. Lockhart et al., The American Constitution, St. Paul: West Publishing Co., 1967.

48. Lowi, Theodore, The End of Liberalism, New York: Norton, 1969.

49. Marshall, Burke, Federalism and Civil Rights, New York, Columbia University Press, 1964.

50. Mason and Garrey (eds.), American Constitutional History, New York: Harper and Row, 1964.

51. McLaughlin, A. C., The Confederation and the Constitution, New York: Harper and Row, 1905.

52. Miller, Charles, The Supreme Court and the Uses of History, Cambridge: Harvard University Press, 1969.

53. Miller, Loren, The Petitioners, New York: Random House Pantheon, 1966.

54. Mitau, G. Theodore, Decade of Decision, New York: Charles Scribner's Sons, 1967.

55. Moynihan and Glazer, Beyond the Melting Pot, Cambridge: M.I.T. Press and Harvard University Press, 1963.

56. "Limiting the Section 1983 Action in the Wake of Monroe v. Pape," Harvard Law Review, Vol. 82, 1969.

57. Phillips, Kevin, The Emerging Republican Majority, New Rochelle, Arlington House, 1969.

58. Radin, Max. "Statutory Interpretation," Harvard Law Review, Vol. 43, 1930.

59. "Reitman v. Mulkey: A Teleophase of Substantive Equal Protection," Supreme Court Review, Chicago: University of Chicago Press, 1967.

60. Report of the National Commission on Civil Disorders, New York: Random House, 1968.

61. Riker, William, Democracy in the United States, New York McMillan Co., 1965.

62. _____, Federalism: Origin, Operation, Significance, Boston: Little, Brown and Co., 1964.

63. Roche, John P. "Civil Liberty in the Age of Enterprise," University of Chicago Law Review, Vol. 31 (1963).

64. _____, Courts and Rights, New York: Random House, 1966.

65. _____, Shadow and Substance, New York: Collier Books, 1964.

66. _____, The Quest for the Dream, New York: McMillan Co., 1963.

67. Shapiro, Martin, Freedom of Speech: The Supreme Court and Judicial Review, Englewood Cliffs, Prentice-Hall, 1966.

68. _____, Law and Politics in the Supreme Court, New York: Free Press, 1964.

69. TenBroek, Jacobus, Equal Under Law, New York: Collier Books, 1965.

70. Truman, David B., The Governmental Process, New York: Alfred Knopf, 1952.

71. Tussman and TenBroek, "The Equal Protection of the Laws," California Law Review, Vol. 37, 1949.

72. Vann Woodward, C., The Strange Career of Jim Crow, New York: Oxford University Press, 1966.

73. Vose, Clement, "Litigation as a Form of Pressure Group Activity," Annals of the American Academy of Political and Social Science, Vol. 319, 1958.

74. Wilson and Banfield, "Public-Regardingness as a Value Premise in Voting Behavior, American Political Science Review, Vol. 58, 1964.

75. Wirt and Hawley, New Directions of Freedom in America San Francisco: Chandler Publishing Co., 1969.

76. Wootton, Graham, Interest-Groups, Englewood Cliffs: Prentice-Hall, 1970.